Radical Love
10 Love Secrets

Randy and Kay McKean

RADICAL LOVE

10 LOVE SECRETS
that will change you, your relationships
and the whole world!

Radical Love—10 Love Secrets

Printed in the United States of America.

ISBN: 978-1-941988-30-5.

Unless otherwise indicated, all Scripture references are from the Holy Bible, New International Version, copyright 1973, 1978, 1984, 2011 by the International Bible Society. Used by permission of Zondervan Bible Publishers.

Cover and interior book design: Toney Mulhollan. The text face is set in Karmina and Proxima Nova.

Copy Editor: Amy Morgan.

Illumination Publishers is committed to caring wisely for God's creation and uses recycled paper whenever possible.

About the authors: Randy McKean was baptized into Christ in 1973 as a student at the University of Florida. He graduated in 1977 achieving a degree in English, Religion and Education with high honors. Kay Summers McKean, raised in Miami, Florida, was baptized into Christ in 1974 and graduated from the University of Florida in 1975 with a degree in Broadcast Journalism. Randy and Kay have served in the full-time ministry for thirty-six years in such diverse locations as Columbia, South Carolina; Tokyo, Japan; Munich, Germany; Paris, France and Boston, Massachusetts. Currently they are serving with the Northern Virginia (NOVA) Church of Christ, where Randy is both lead evangelist and an elder and Kay is the director of women's ministries.

While leading in Boston from 1990 to 2003, Randy and Kay simultaneously prepared and led mission teams to Europe. Randy is the author of the book *Radical Faith—10 Faith Secrets*. Kay has written the book, *Our Beginning* and coauthored *Love Your Husband*. Both have also been editor and contributor for multiauthored book projects. Randy and Kay have been married for thirty-nine years and have two married children and four grandchildren. For more information about their ministry go to www.nvcoc.org. For more information about their writing go to www.facebook.com/RandyandKayMcKean.

ILLUMINATION PUBLISHERS

www.ipibooks.com
6010 Pinecreek Ridge Court
Spring, Texas 77379-2513

CONTENTS

DEDICATION

This book is dedicated to our parents:
Rear Admiral Thomas Wayne McKean
Marilyn Ruth Kimberlin McKean
Nancy Katherine Payne Summers
and to the memory of Robert Steinmetz Summers
YOU LOVED US FIRST!

ACKNOWLEDGMENTS

We would like to say a huge "thank-you" for the love, support and encouragement of the Northern Virginia Church of Christ, where we have had the privilege and honor of serving in the ministry for the past ten years. Your love for God is obvious. We think you are amazing!

The illustrations are by Kevin F. J. Harris. He's a year-old brother who serves with all his heart! Thank you for your help.

PREFACE

Dear friends, let us love one another, for love comes from God. Everyone who loves has been born of God and knows God. Whoever does not love does not know God, because God is love. This is how God showed his love among us: He sent his one and only Son into the world that we might live through him. This is love: not that we loved God, but that he loved us and sent his Son as an atoning sacrifice for our sins. Dear friends, since God so loved us, we also ought to love one another. No one has ever seen God; but if we love one another, God lives in us and his love is made complete in us.

1 John 4:7–12

We all want to love and be loved. Everyone is interested in love. Everyone is searching for love. Everyone is longing for love. Everyone wants to know more about love. We dream about it. We see movies about it. We read books about it. We sing about it. The majority of songs on the radio are either about falling in love or falling out of love. Whether it be the 1956 Nat King Cole song "When I Fall in Love"; Elvis Presley's 1961 song, "Can't Help Falling in Love"; the Beatles' 1967 song, "All You Need Is Love"; Peter Frampton's 1975 "Baby I Love Your Way"; Air Supply's 1980 "All Out of Love"; the Whitney Houston 1992 hit "I Will Always Love You"; the upbeat 2003 Beyoncé song "Crazy in Love"; or, now in 2016, Justin Bieber's "Love Yourself"—in every decade there are songs about love. But how many people really experience love to the degree we were created to experience it?

People are frustrated because of disappointing loves. People are hurting because of failures in love. People are scared to love because of past hurts. And what happens when a person gets hurt? Some pull into themselves and become quiet. They slowly numb themselves to their pain. They bury themselves in work and hobbies. Others explode by getting angry or drunk. Others try to get back at the person or persons who have hurt them. They may not talk to them or they may just ignore them as inside they hate and despise them. Some may go so far as to have sex with someone else (maybe with someone they hardly know!) to cause the pain they feel to be felt in turn by the one they once said they loved. In the end, all of this leaves a person empty, fearful, sarcastic and pessimistic about love.

A life without love tears a person up inside. We were created for love. People must have love or they cease to really live—they start to just exist. Love is essential, not optional. But here's the problem: Most people live only with an illusion of love. They either dream about love in the past, which is usually better in their memory than it was in reality, or they dream about love that's just around the next corner. The truth is that people are lonely and scared. They are looking for love in all the wrong places and in all the wrong faces. Marriages are not working, as the average marriage lasts no more than six years. For too many people, love does not endure and does not satisfy. Why? Because people are not connected with the author of love. God is love. All people will experience bits and pieces of love in this world but they will find it wanting until they intimately know God and allow him to define love.

For us, writing a book about love is a daunting task. We are far from being perfect examples of love, but we have dedicated our lives to following the perfect example of love. We are very aware of the ways we have loved imperfectly. We have at times shown impatience, frustration, arrogance or neglect. But any failure on our part does not void God's perfect love or his words about love! In fact, the process of writing a book on love has, for us, renewed the great Bible challenge to love others more and more (1 Thessalonians 4:9–10). We started the process of writing this book by reading every passage in the Bible that uses the word "love." That was very enlightening and exhilarating!

So why write a book on love? Because there is so much confusion about it. It's like the time that four people were traveling in a small train compartment in the Wild West. An old lady and a beautiful young lady were seated facing a crusty general and his aide, a handsome lieutenant. All of a sudden they went through a long tunnel that made their compartment pitch black. In the darkness, they heard the sound of a loud kiss, followed by the sound of a slap. Now that's a confusing situation.

The old lady was thinking: *That terrible lieutenant! He kissed this sweet, innocent girl and then she slapped him.*

The young woman was thinking: *That poor lieutenant! He tried to kiss me (and that would have been so nice!) and missed and kissed the old lady instead and she slapped him.*

The general was thinking: *I can't believe it! (rubbing his cheek) My aide kissed this beautiful girl and in trying to slap him, she slapped me instead!*

The lieutenant was thinking: *I can't believe it! (while smiling) I've waited a long time for an opportunity like this and it finally came!* (He had kissed the back of his hand and then slapped the general's face!)

Yes, everyone except the lieutenant was quite confused! When it comes to love, it seems that everyone's got an opinion, an idea, a blog, a newspaper story, a book, a song, a magazine article, a tweet or a Facebook comment with some kind of advice about it. And yet, people are in the dark and find themselves guessing when it comes to love. The only one who really knows what love is and how love is to be manifested in our lives is God himself. It cannot be said too many times: God is love. This is his very essence. This is to be our very essence.

This book is for believers who need to more fully understand what this wonderful thing called love is and how it can work in our lives in concrete and practical ways. This is not a book on marriage, although it will help any marriage. It is for every Christian who wants to love better and love deeper. This is not a "touchy-feely" book about sentimental love. Reading it will require not only your heart but your intellect, as we will cover some challenging and often misunderstood topics. It is hoped that those who read this book will be fully invested in the quest to love in the way God calls us to love.

For too many, the concept of love remains ethereal and confusing. We are given new lives when we are forgiven of all our sins, but we bring a lot of baggage from our old lives into our new ones. Unlearning what the world has taught us about love can be challenging. Learning how to love God and how to love others is a lifetime endeavor. The old must be replaced with the new at the beginning of our Christian lives and the process must continue throughout our

Christian lives.

As individuals, as church congregations, and as a universal fellowship of churches, we must grow in our capacity to love. In fact, we need a cultural evolution that takes us to levels of love we have never been to before! Our love must be evolving into a better and greater love. Love is positive. It is the most positive force in the universe! Our Christian relationships and our Christian churches should be the most positive environments on earth that shout, scream and cry out affirmation, respect, appreciation, forgiveness, encouragement and acceptance along with the upward call and expectation to become more like Christ. People are to feel loved. People are to be cared for and protected at their most vulnerable times in life. People are to be inspired and called higher. People are to feel safe and believed in. We must never be the Christian relationship or the church that mirrors the words of the T-shirt that reads: "The beatings will continue until morale improves!" We get beat up by the world every day; therefore, we must get built up by the church every day. It is an unhealthy environment that leaves people feeling they are always in trouble or they are never good enough or they never do enough. People can't thrive or stay in a negative environment. We need to be the people who are great at catching people in what they're doing right instead of what they're doing wrong. Love is to draw people to the truth. Love is to keep people in the truth. Authentic love is up-building and positive. The world is to recognize us because of this love.

Through our years of following Jesus, we have learned love secrets as revealed in the Bible that have revolutionized our lives and the lives of those around us. It doesn't matter where a person lives or what their background is, love changes lives. We have lived in the northern United States, the southern United States, in Asia and in Europe. We have traveled to over fifty countries around the world. We have had the honor and the privilege of teaching people about God's love and we are always amazed every time a person's life is transformed by love. This book promises to unveil how to live a life of love. Some of the things you'll learn are how to have the right kind of self-love; how to have loving discernment that allows tremendous impact on people's lives; how to have maximum sexual love; and how to have friendships that protect, expect and make life fun. These principles or secrets are what we have built healthy and growing ministries on, and they have given great satisfaction, fulfillment and enjoyment to our personal lives as well. We know they can do the same for you in your life. The results promise to be RADICAL!

In 1994, during the thirteen-year period in which we had the joy and privilege to lead the great missions-focused Boston Church of Christ, we planned a celebration of the congregation's fifteenth birthday. We rented the historical Boston Garden. We had an enormous birthday cake made to feed the thousands in attendance. We had hundreds of multicolored balloons that would drop down on the congregation to make the celebration complete. And we entitled the event Radical Love. We asked our talented music director to write a song using this title as a tribute to what had been done through the love of God and through the love of the Boston Church. The song became a theme song for churches around the world. Years later my son and his wife put some new words to the song while keeping the powerful words of the chorus the same. As we (Randy and Kay) continue to grow in love, our hope is that the things we have learned will spur others on to obey the two greatest commands: to love God and to love others. As disciples around the world do this, God will do amazing things because of his RADICAL LOVE that results in our RADICAL LOVE.

RADICAL LOVE

Lyrics by Robert Duncan, ©2002 RobDuncanMusic/ASCAP

Additional lyrics by Kent and Heather McKean

It started 2,000 years ago
When God came down to earth;
In a little town called Bethlehem
A virgin girl gave birth.
God with us in human form
Was born to give us worth,
And the news rang out
To be heard around the world.

Now thirty years they came and went;
That boy grew to a man.
Our Lord began to preach about
His Father's master plan.
They broke him down and hung him up;
God raised him from the ground,
And then they made their vow
To turn the whole world "upside down"!

It's a radical love that we share.
Oh, it's a love that's heard around the world
And it shows how much God cares.
It's a radical love around the world,
A love that we keep multiplying
Every time we go and preach the Word.

Centuries have come and gone,
And look what God has done!
We've spread into the nations now,
And we've only just begun.
What started in Jerusalem
Is preached around the world;
It's a radical love
And it's up to us to make it heard!

It's a radical love that we share.
Oh, it's a love that's heard around the world
And it shows how much God cares.
It's a radical love around the world,
A love that we keep multiplying
Every time we go and preach the Word.

It's a radical love that we share.
Oh, it's a love that's heard around the world
And it shows how much God cares.

rad-i-cal adj 3a: marked by a considerable departure from the usual or traditional: EXTREME b: tending or disposed to make extreme changes in existing views, habits, conditions or institutions.

—Merriam Webster's Collegiate Dictionary, Tenth Edition

PART ONE

GOD IS LOVE

Who is God? What is God? Where is God? These are questions asked daily across the globe. Because you are reading this book, you may feel like you already have the answer. Perhaps you have chosen to believe in God, to trust in him and to give your life to him. Yet even those of faith ponder the complexity of really knowing God. In times of darkness and doubt, the questions return. And even if you are settled in your own mind, you want to be able to clearly assist others on their journey of faith. You want to know...

Who Is the Lord?

Thousands of years ago, this question was on the mind of the most powerful man alive. In ancient Egypt, this man had built a civilization by the sweat and toil of slaves from the Hebrew race. Moses, a Hebrew by birth but raised in the same palace as this powerful man, came with a message for him. It wasn't a request or a favor, but a command: *"Let my people go."* Moses made it clear that it was the Lord, the God of Israel, who commanded the release of the Hebrews. And then Pharaoh spoke: *"Who is the Lord, that I should obey him...? I do not know the Lord"* (Exodus 5:2).

We are worlds away from Pharaoh's irreverent statement, and yet his declaration could be echoed by millions in our generation: "Who is God? Why should I obey him? I do not know God." These words are repeated in various ways, not only by those who do not profess to know God, but even by those who do.

Through the centuries, many have sought to answer Pharaoh's question, striving to help their fellow man know who God is. *"God is love"*: this is the simplest and truest description of God. Yet the challenge remains because not only does the human race have a hard time conceiving of God, they also find it difficult or impossible to know love.

Let's go back again to the time of Moses and see how God describes himself. Several years after his interaction with Pharaoh, we find Moses on Mount Sinai, ready to receive the second set of stone tablets inscribed with God's law. It is in this scene that we see God defining himself with these words: *"The Lord, the Lord, the compassionate and gracious God, slow to anger, abounding in love and faithfulness, maintaining love to thousands, and forgiving wickedness, rebellion and sin"* (Exodus 34:6-7a).

God knows who he is. He doesn't change his mind or his character. The way he introduced himself to Moses is the way he introduces himself to you and me today. God is *still* love.

Think about it. If someone asks you, "Who are you?" your immediate answer would include your name and maybe where you live or what your job is. But if the person persisted in asking, "Who are you?" then you might pause, consider, and describe yourself in words a bit more precise. You would perhaps describe your family, your hobbies, even your religion or political beliefs. But let's say this inquisitive person continued to press you for more detail: "Who are you?" Only then (and only if you were willing) would you convey the deepest part of yourself. You would reveal your heart.

This is what God did with Moses on Mount Sinai, and it's what he's doing now with us. When we read in the Bible that God is love, we are seeing God's heart, his character, who he is. Love is what defines his personality and his actions. "Ah," you say, "but what about the wrath of God, and the anger of God, and the jealousy of God? That's in the Bible too, isn't it?" Yes indeed, God allows us to see those elements of his nature. However, to most of us, anger and jealousy arise out of sinful and selfish intentions of the heart, so we don't understand them in the loving God. God's anger is always a response of love. His nature is protective love, and when sinful actions occur that cause damage, his anger is revealed. His "jealous" love is not a vindictive or victimized jealousy, but a response to the betrayal of the beloved, whether it's an individual or a nation. The purpose is always the same: a desire to awaken within the sinner a longing to return to God. If God didn't have a "jealous" love for us, then wouldn't we doubt how much he loves us? *"Or do you think Scripture says without reason that he jealously longs for the spirit he has caused to dwell in us?"* (James 4:5).

God's discipline is also an act of love:

"My son, do not make light of the Lord's discipline,
and do not lose heart when he rebukes you,
because the Lord disciplines the one he loves,
and he chastens everyone he accepts as his son."
(Hebrews 12:5–6; see Proverbs 3:12)

C.S. Lewis wrote: "Love may forgive all infirmities and love still in spite of them, but Love cannot cease to will their removal." In other words, God will love us enough to make sure that anything harmful or dishonorable will be eliminated. He wants the best for us always, even if the best that he seeks might only be revealed through trials or suffering.

"The Lord, the Lord, abounding in faithfulness and love..." Love is the supreme quality in all God does. This description of God runs like a thread through the entire Old Testament. The psalmists and the prophets repeat the same words, but our favorite example is found in the book of Jonah.

When we talk about Jonah, what is the first thing that pops into your mind? Usually, it's "Jonah was swallowed by a whale." First of all, let's remember that Jonah was not technically swallowed by a whale. After he was thrown into the sea by terrified sailors during a horrific storm, the Bible says that the Lord provided a huge *fish* to swallow Jonah. A whale is a mammal. A fish is...a fish!

Being swallowed by a fish doesn't seem like a pleasant event, but notice that the Lord *provided* the fish. Just because scientists today can't find any evidence of a whale or fish that would be able to swallow a human being whole doesn't mean that God couldn't have provided one for that very purpose. And understand that it's precisely because Jonah was swallowed that his life was saved. The fish was an underwater life preserver.

But there's so much more to Jonah than this. After he finally agreed to God's command to preach to the Ninevites (the hated enemy of his people), Jonah still didn't "get" God. He invoked the exact same words that Moses had heard so many years before: *"I knew that you are a gracious and compassionate God, slow to anger and abounding in love..."* yet he was profoundly disappointed that God did not destroy Nineveh at that time. The final chapter of Jonah solidifies the description that even Jonah himself misunderstood.

Jonah went outside the city, pouting and hoping beyond hope that even though the people of the city had deeply repented of their evil deeds, somehow God would go ahead and wipe them out. While he sat and sulked, God *provided* a plant to grow over him and protect him from the heat. Jonah was happy about that plant, mysteriously creeping up around his hastily erected hut. Just as Jonah began to feel comforted about things not going his way, God *provided* a worm to eat the plant so that it withered. Wouldn't you like to have seen that worm? Think something off the screen of *Aliens*: jagged teeth dripping with wicked venom, slimy skin with scales that cut through the dirt. It could have been like that! Then God *provided* a scorching wind while the sun blazed on Jonah's head. Perhaps Jonah was thinking: "Really, Lord? I came out of the gut of a stinky fish to be blasted by this heat? I think I'll faint. Better yet, just let me die." It is here that God finally intervened, speaking kindly to the despondent Jonah, and showing him what "love" means. Jonah's concern for his plant was nothing compared to God's concern for the human souls in the city of Nineveh. *"And should I not have concern for the great city of Nineveh, in which there are more than a hundred and twenty thousand people who cannot tell their right hand from the left—and also many animals?"*

That final sentence in the book of Jonah puts it all together. God has concern. Some scholars speculate that the number he specifies refers solely to the children of the city—those who cannot tell their right hand from the left. Whether this is true or not, it is certain that God cares for the people of Nineveh. And not only for the people but even for the animals! All that God had done for Jonah, all that he provided for him, would eventually teach not only Jonah but you and me the extent God will go to in order to show us his love.

The book of Jonah gives us an example to learn who God is and what love is. The words of Jesus many years later resonate with similar conviction: *"Are not two sparrows sold for a penny? Yet not one of them will fall to the ground apart from the will of the Father. And even the very hairs of your head are all numbered. So don't be afraid; you are worth more than many sparrows"* (Matthew 10:29–31).

KAY: I always claim that this is the scripture that converted me. As a college student in the 1970s, I was doing all I could to "find myself." That search included self-evaluation, writing in journals, dabbling in drugs, self-expression and sexual "freedom." Yet I found that self-worth and self-knowledge were vague and beyond my reach. I was finally persuaded by friends to read the Bible, but even that became a halfhearted effort to be more spiritual. I approached the Scriptures with cynicism, until my eyes fastened on the words of Jesus: "Even the hairs of your head are all numbered." In all my searching for myself, I acknowledged that I could not know myself as well as God knew me. In all of my self-examination, both on the outside with a mirror and on the inside with introspection, I still couldn't know how many hairs were on my head! No one, not even my hairdresser, could give me a precise count. But God could, because he knows me. Jesus' statement did it for me—a vague and impersonal God suddenly became real and intimate. From that point on, I knew I was a changed woman. If it's true that God created me and knows me that intimately, what could I do but devote my life to knowing him? Since that time, I have continued to make it my goal to know God and to make him known to others.

Do you know how many hairs are on your head? OK, for some it might be easier, the hairs have been steadily falling out through the years so there are fewer left to count. But in reality no one knows how many hairs are on their head. Scientists have produced numbers, but they are not exact and they are not individual. But God knows. What does this tell you? God knows you better than you know yourself.

Love begins with knowing and caring. That's what God does. That's who God is. We can't really continue with the rest of God's character of love until we see this first. In order for us to be convinced that God loves us, we must understand that he knows us.

The French language has two words for the word we use as "know": *savoir* and *connaître*. Savoir has to do with knowing about something or knowing how to do something. *"Je sais cuisiner"* ("I know how to cook"). The word connaître is more about knowing a person or being familiar with a place. *"Je connais Amy"* ("I know Amy"). When we speak of God knowing us, we could use both words. He knows all about us, and he is also intimately aware of who we are. He has met us. He is familiar with us. This is a great gift, if we really think about it. The God of the universe and of all created things has a familiarity with you. He is aware of every hair on your head and every thought in your mind.

"Nothing in all creation is hidden from God. Everything is naked and exposed before his eyes" (Hebrews 4:13 NLT). Is this statement good news or bad news to you? While some may look at those words with some anxiety, it is primarily a reassuring message. God knows you perfectly. He is not an impersonal deity. He longs for a relationship with you because he *knows* (*connaît*) you!

God has known you from the time of your conception. In fact, God has even known you long before you were a twinkle in your father's eye! Scripture teaches us that God foreknew every person and had a plan for each one. This is hard, impossible really, for us to grasp. Our finite minds can't comprehend how well God knows us. It's one of those things we must accept by faith. Once we accept this, we can move on to accepting the fact that he also loves us.

Establishing the fact that his love begins by knowing us, we must go on to seeing what the qualities of love are like. The song "I Want to Know What Love Is" by Foreigner is ringing in our ears right now! Again, God has not left us clueless about the meaning of love.

One of the most well-known scriptures on love is found in 1 Corinthians 13. This passage is read at weddings, funerals, and any event when heartstrings need to be pulled. It's a beautiful description of love:

Love is patient,
Love is kind.
It does not envy,
It does not boast, it is not proud.
It does not dishonor others,
It is not self-seeking,
It is not easily angered,
It keeps no record of wrongs.
Love does not delight in evil but rejoices with the truth.
It always protects,
Always trusts,
Always hopes,
Always perseveres.
Love never fails.

These words define love, and in so doing, they define God.

KAY: *There are lots of reasons why I love this passage, but one of them has to do with an incident that occurred a year or so after I became a Christian. A friend of mine had been adamantly opposed to Christianity. She was not open at all to studying the Bible, although she was open to friendship and "hanging out" from time to time, and she respected my life and the lives of others in our church fellowship. At the time, I was single, living in an apartment with several other young women, and my friend came to visit. I had been reading my Bible and it had remained open on the kitchen table, with 1 Corinthians 13 in plain view. It was not my intention at all to "show off" this passage; it was simply there. While we chatted and I prepared food in the kitchen, my friend glanced down at the Bible and began to read silently. Suddenly I noticed that she became transfixed by the page, and her eyes began to well with tears. "This is it," she said softly. "This is what I want." From that instant she opened her heart to learning about God's love. She became a believer in Jesus and was baptized into Christ not too long afterward. The love of God is powerful —even when you least expect it!*

RANDY: *One of the best things I have ever done in my spiritual life was to spend thirty days of quiet times on these passages about love. I was two years old as a disciple. I knew that I needed to grow in love big-time. I knew that I had only the world's concept of love given to me (brainwashed from songs, books and movies!) for many years with only some sprinkling of the right understanding of love, so I decided to really go after it. I bought books on God's love and on developing Christian love. I memorized 1 Corinthians chapter 13 bit by bit. I studied out each word about love mentioned in these passages. I prayed about knowing what love is and to become more loving. My eyes were opened a great deal during that time and I became a very different person because of developing that focus for my life. Obviously, I didn't come close to knowing all about love in thirty days. Growing in love is a lifetime endeavor. But I had started on the greatest journey in life!*

GOD IS PATIENT

The word patience (in Greek, *makrothumein*) describes a person who has been offended in some way by another person, and yet does not show retribution. This person could easily avenge but chooses not to do so. The old-fashioned way of saying it is "long-suffering." God's love means that he is patient with us. He suffers along with us as we stumble through life with our mistakes and failures. He doesn't throw up his hands and give up, but continues to pick us up and guide us through the maze of everyday living.

GOD IS KIND

Kindness is the act of doing good for another. It is motivated from or characterized by sympathy. A kind act is useful for the benefit of another. God's kindness is seen every day, if we will only stop and acknowledge it. The air we breathe, the food we eat, the life we have are all because of the fact that God is kind.

GOD DOES NOT ENVY

Envy is characterized by being resentful of what another person has. Since God is the giver of all good things, he rejoices in the blessings that we enjoy. He does not wish to take away good things, but wants us to recognize that all good things come from him.

GOD DOES NOT BOAST AND IS NOT PROUD

God will not force himself on anyone. He is a gentleman. Even in his great power and magnificence, there is no arrogance in him.

GOD DOES NOT DISHONOR OTHERS

God's greatest desire is to help his people live lives of honor and glory. All that he does is to bring us higher and closer to him. He is not demeaning or belittling in his work with the human race. Although God is higher and greater, he shows gentleness and humility to us. As some translations tell it, he has stooped down to make us great (Psalm 18:35).

GOD IS NOT SELF-SEEKING

If God were a self-seeking god, he would have given up on us long ago. His character is just the opposite of that. He seeks to serve others. From the beginning of time, all of his interactions with mankind have been for our benefit. Although it has been complained that we must play by "God's rules," in reality God's ways are best for every human creature.

GOD IS NOT EASILY ANGERED

Thank goodness for that! We don't have to live in a state of constant panic that God is irritated with us. Because he understands our weaknesses, he doesn't "fly off the handle" when we fail. It's not to say that God knows no anger, but his definition is quite different from our own. The petty difficulties of life don't disrupt his demeanor as they do ours.

GOD KEEPS NO RECORD OF WRONGS

Scripture abounds with examples of how God treats our sins when we have repented and come to him in faith. They are removed from us *"as far as the east is from the west."* They will be remembered no more (Hebrews 8:12). He does not count our sins against us (2 Corinthians 5:19). And our favorite: he hurls them into the depths of the sea (Micah 7:19). This is an important truth for those of us who like to go deep-sea fishing for our sins: God wants to wipe the slate clean. He desires to give us a fresh start every day.

GOD DOES NOT DELIGHT IN EVIL
BUT REJOICES WITH THE TRUTH

God finds no pleasure in anything that is wrong. He has no joy in seeing tragedy or evil. His greatest pleasure is when good people do good things. Every act of kindness brings him a smile. In all the sufferings of life, God looks for a way to provide good.

GOD ALWAYS PROTECTS

The word "protects" figuratively refers to "a roof over." We might regard a "helicopter parent" with amusement or disdain, but when it comes to God, it's good to know that he hovers over us always. He watches out for us individually at all times.

GOD ALWAYS TRUSTS

Trust means assuming the best about someone, not the worst. In his love, God looks at each of us with the eyes of trust. He knows there is something good in us, even when others or even we ourselves doubt it.

GOD ALWAYS HOPES

There is an expectation that God has for our lives. He created us in love to become someone fantastic. His hope for us is not a meager last-ditch effort. On the contrary, his hopes and dreams for us are bigger than we can imagine. Others may give up on you, but God always hopes!

GOD ALWAYS PERSEVERES

When so many things and people in our lives quit, God remains. In all our relationships and occupations and efforts, God is the only one who will never let us down. His perseverance is not passive but is active with strength and determination.

GOD NEVER FAILS

This is the most significant description of love, and this describes God perfectly. Failing, in this context, means to be driven off course or to become inefficient. A failure is one who loses his way. God will not "fall away." God never wanders, and God is never lost. He never forgets who he is. God is love. "And so we know and rely on the love God has for us. God is love. Whoever lives in love lives in God, and God in them" (1 John 4:16).

God is love, but can he prove it? Yes, yes and yes. God has proven that he is love by conceiving of a plan that would change the world.

We all know the story of *"in the beginning."* Adam and Eve enjoyed this God of love until they began to doubt that he had their best interests at heart. They listened to the lie that God was holding out on them. Although they were given everything they needed for life and enjoyment, they took it upon themselves to see if God was telling them the truth.

When Adam and Eve took that first heartbreaking bite into sin, they set the stage for all who would follow in their steps. Ultimately, they were expelled from their paradise and suffered the hardships of life and death. But even in that painful ordeal, God's love was still made known. The very first promise of a redeemer—a rescuer from sin—was given (Genesis 3:15). And when Adam and Eve made a shambles of trying to cover up their shame with fig leaves, God came in and made a covering that would foreshadow something far into the future: a sacrifice of love.

God is love, and he proved it when he provided a perfect representative of himself to the world. God's ultimate expression of love is giving us Jesus. This is the proof, the testimony, the confirmation of his love for us. What more evidence do we need to believe that God is love? *"For God so loved the world that he gave his one and only Son, that whoever believes in him shall not perish but have eternal life"* (John 3:16).

Stop for just a moment and tell yourself something very profound and exciting. Say to yourself: "You are lovable!" Do you believe it? Say it again; you might not have been listening the first time! Say it and believe that it's a fact. It must be true, because the Bible says so:

> *This is how God showed his love among us: He sent his one and only Son into the world that we might live through him. This is love: not that we loved God, but that he loved us and sent his Son as an atoning sacrifice for our sins.* (1 John 4:9–10)

You are so lovable that God sent Jesus into this world to let you know it!

What does it take to convince you that you are loved? Expressions of sentiment? Extravagant gifts? The ultimate test of love is to be willing to die for the beloved. This was the sacrifice Jesus made. This is the evidence of God's love.

God's love is radical. It's extreme. It's unusual. It's uncompromising. It's drastic. It's exciting. It's profound.

And it's real.

Amazingly, we can live in this kind of love every day. God wants this for you even more than you want it for yourself. He's done everything to show you this love, and he simply wants you to soak it up, enjoy it and share it with others.

Can you do that? Deeply knowing at our intellectual and emotional core that GOD IS LOVE is only the beginning of the life-changing journey of radical love. As you continue in the following chapters, you will delve into what it means to live in, live by and live for God's amazing RADICAL LOVE!

So hold on tight and enjoy the ride!

PART TWO

JESUS REVEALS LOVE

- In the land of Palestine many years ago, a certain widow's son was her only source of comfort and security. She is proud of her young man, who will care for her as she ages. But then the unspeakable occurs. Through illness or injury, the young man dies. She is alone.

- A foreign woman, an outcast among the people of the land, clings to her daughter for company and love. But strangely, the young girl recently has changed. Her personality is twisted, and her behavior is bizarre. The woman has nowhere to turn.

- A young man, full of potential and vitality, enjoys his youth along with his friends. The future is open for them. But one day, his destiny has been destroyed. His body is broken; he can no longer move and must be carried about on a pallet. His friends are there for him, but what can they do?

- A man who has lived his whole life in the darkness is under suspicion for his condition. His eyes have never beheld the light of day. Even his parents are aloof. His handicap is the topic of philosophical discussions, but the talking does nothing to improve his circumstances.

These are all "hopeless" cases, full of tragedy. The sadness exuding from each of these individuals' lives is palpable. Their lives are empty and desperate. What can possibly happen to change these despairing souls?

Jesus can happen. Jesus burst into the lives of each of these people, transforming their worlds into brightness. The blind man was given sight, and answers were given about his suffering. The paralyzed man can walk, giving his friends great joy and astonishment. The foreigner's daughter was healed, and she herself was held up as a beacon for all. And the widow's son returned to life and all those around her proclaim: *"God has come to help his people"* (Luke 7:16).

Yes, truly, God had come, in the person of Jesus, to help his people. These people and countless others were the recipients of God's help as Jesus went from town to town, teaching, healing, feeding and nourishing the souls of men and women. Why? Because he came to show them love. He came to show them God.

God certainly revealed himself in many ways before the time of Christ. God commissioned men and women to get his message out, beginning as early as the time of Noah, that *"preacher of righteousness"* (2 Peter 2:5).

> *In the past God spoke to our ancestors through the prophets at many times and in various ways, but in these last days he has spoken to us by his Son, whom he appointed heir of all things, and through whom also he made the universe.*
>
> *The Son is the radiance of God's glory and the exact representation of his being, sustaining all things by his powerful word. After he had provided purification for sins, he sat down at the right hand of the Majesty in heaven.* (Hebrews 1:1–3)

All the prophets and spokesmen and women of God were giving a glimpse of who God is. When Jesus came, he provided a real, multidimensional, flesh-and-blood manifestation of the living God. The prophets came with a whisper; Jesus came with a shout.

A Love-Revealing Life

When you are asked how God shows his love through Jesus, your immediate answer might be this: "Jesus died for me." How true that is. But let's take it back a bit, before that earth-shattering death. Let's go back several years, to the time when we see, in our mind's eye, the beginning of God's love revealed.

Inside the dark womb of a young woman, an embryo begins to grow. From that embryo, a fetus develops, a male child. He kicks and stretches to make room for his body to grow. He relies on the woman for nourishment and life. He is jostled along as his mother travels close to the time of birth. Finally, at just the right time, he squeezes through the narrow birth canal and drops into the arms of a man who will raise him to manhood.

The infant draws his first breath in a stable of animals and takes his nourishment from his teenage mother. After a few days, he is subjected to circumcision and to the speculation of the curious. He is bustled away to a foreign land to escape being slaughtered, until he is finally able to make his home in an outpost village of a conquered nation.

Jesus learns to crawl, and with many scrapes and bruises, he learns to walk. His first words are a jumble of sounds, until he finally can articulate in the language of his family. He plays games with relatives and friends, learns his numbers and his letters and does his household chores. He studies the Torah and travels miles for religious festivals.

Jesus grows up and becomes a man. His body is acquainted with hunger, thirst and fatigue. He is exposed to temptation. He feels rejection and loneliness. He also feels joy and knows laughter. He lives.

Living is *hard*. And Jesus was willing to *live* so that he could reveal the love of God to us.

When we consider what *could* have occurred, what God deserved, we realize what a sacrifice he made. Angels could have transported a fully grown Son of God to the earth, revealing his power and magnificence for the entire world to see. He could have forced all the inhabitants of the world to bow down to his eminence. If he had to die, he could have been subjected to a quick, painless execution, without torture or disgrace. But then how would we realize the extent of his love? No, Jesus lived to show us his love.

We jokingly talk about our "first-world problems" (What? No

lightning-fast Internet? You've got to be kidding!), yet Jesus willingly lived in what would be considered a third world nation with primitive conditions. The Broadway musical *Jesus Christ Superstar* presents Judas' complaint to Jesus in a song, lamenting his choice of "such a backward time" and "such a strange land." Jesus was willing to live his life in an environment that was not easy or luxurious.

Don't move on to the next thoughts about how Jesus reveals love until you fully comprehend this one. When you go through the typical struggles of life, as every human being does on the face of this swirling globe, remember that Jesus had to deal with these daily troubles too. Consider the humility it took for him to be just a "normal man" during his early years. He had to learn a trade, and we assume he was a carpenter, like Joseph. Imagine: the Son of God taking an order for a table. The Savior of the world dealing with a difficult customer. The Messiah hauling timber from a supplier.

Jesus had to learn to prepare the wood, to measure and construct the products. He had to deal with people, both customers and possibly coworkers. He faced financial pressures and deadlines. Jesus knew and understood the life of a working man. His religious training and his professional training were all part of what Jesus had to learn as the Son of Man. Those aspects of his young life prepared him for his ministry. Jesus could relate to those he taught because he had walked in their shoes. He could identify with the everyday, average person and could speak to their needs. He spent most of his life doing the "ordinary" things before he did the extraordinary things. The humanness of Jesus reveals his love for you and me.

A Love-Revealing Parable

Jesus' earthly ministry was the backdrop for doing what he came to do. As he gathered followers, he began to teach. Often, he spoke in parables, stories that anyone could understand if they had *"ears to hear."* His parables—earthly stories with heavenly meanings—addressed various issues, but ultimately they all pointed their hearers to the love of God.

But Jesus' parables were not meant simply to entertain. They were told to inspire change. He was the master of giving visual examples that would ultimately make a difference in people's lives. He was the best kind of teacher.

Today, we long for teachers who will have the wisdom and finesse to change attitudes and behavior. We heard of that kind of teaching provided by a principal in a school near Washington DC. She had a unique dilemma on her hands. Some of the young girls in the middle school were experimenting with lipstick for the first time, and they would congregate in the bathroom to try it out. Nothing wrong with that, except that then they would press their lips on the bathroom mirror. Dozens of little lip prints would remain on the mirror until the maintenance man arrived every evening to clean them off. The next day, there they were again, and again the maintenance man had to work to remove them. This became such a problem for him that the principal finally decided to do something about it. She called all the girls into the bathroom and had them stand before the mirror with the maintenance man. When she explained the difficulty that he had in removing the lip prints every evening, the girls were not impressed. The principal could tell that her admonitions would not make a difference. So she finally asked the maintenance man to show the girls how much effort was required in cleaning the mirror. He took out a long handled squeegee, dipped it in the toilet, and cleaned the mirror. From that point on, there were no lip prints on the mirror. You see, the girls had to see things from a different perspective! That's what a good educator does.

In one set of Jesus' parables, he tells of a shepherd who climbs over hill and vale, searching for a lost sheep. Then he speaks of a woman who is on her hands and knees searching for a lost coin. And last, he depicts a father yearning for his wayward son (Luke 15:3–24).

Many artists have depicted the little wandering sheep as a delicate and soft lamb, its "fleece as white as snow." Little do they know that when a sheep is separated from the flock and the shepherd, its appearance is anything but sweet. A lone sheep is in danger from predators, in danger from parasites, dehydrated and malnourished.

The coin, although not technically in danger, has great value, but the value can never be claimed in its hidden state. Like a $100 bill hidden behind the cushions in your sofa, the coin is worthless until it is found.

The son has wandered from the father and has fallen into a life of waste.

What do the sheep, the coin and the son have in common? They are all lost. What do the shepherd, the woman and the father have in common? They are all images that Jesus gives to show God's love. The searching shepherd, the woman on her knees, and the father longing for his son illustrate God and his desire for us. Jesus didn't use these images lightly. He wants us to know that this is how we must see God! Later, Jesus would take this parable to another level when he claimed that he is the Good Shepherd, who lays down his life for the sheep. He didn't just tell the story, he lived it.

We often talk about the fact that we have a responsibility to seek God. That is absolutely true. Remember, though, that you can never seek him more than he is seeking for a relationship with you. God is not passively waiting for you to find him. *"He is not far from any one of us"* (Acts 17:27).

Jesus' parables were remembered, and they have brought about healing, repentance, inspiration and change to millions of lives. He reveals love by his stories, and those stories radically alter the lives of those who hear them. He is our beloved rabbi and the master Teacher.

KAY: If the goal of the game Hide and Seek is to not be found, why is it that the moment of finding is so deliciously thrilling and fun? At least that's what I've discovered when I play. When I hide in the closet behind clothes and shoes, folding my whole body into a tight ball to conceal myself the best I can, and then hear the footsteps of little children coming in, pausing, then with little hands pushing back the clothes to reveal their grandmother crouched on the floor, there is a shriek of delight from both the children and from me. When the game is reversed, I count to twenty-five, wander the house, and then hear giggles and shuffles, making my job as the seeker easy. Still, I give them good time to enjoy hiding behind the shower curtain before I swish it aside to find smiles and laughter and hugs. What a fun game!

When we read the Bible and pray, we are seeking God and his will in our lives. Each Scripture reading is like a pulling back of a curtain, revealing the God who wants to be found. He is not hiding from us, but is making himself known through his word, his creation and his people. But consider this: we sometimes think we are doing all the hard work in our act of seeking God. Truthfully, it's God who is actively seeking us! Whether or not we are hiding intentionally or unintentionally, God is searching for us and waiting for that instant when he can say: "I found you!"

A Love-Revealing Courtroom

At dawn he appeared again in the temple courts, where all the people gathered around him, and he sat down to teach them. The teachers of the law and the Pharisees brought in a woman caught in adultery. They made her stand before the group and said to Jesus, "Teacher, this woman was caught in the act of adultery. In the Law Moses commanded us to stone such women. Now what do you say?" They were using this question as a trap, in order to have a basis for accusing him.

But Jesus bent down and started to write on the ground with his finger. When they kept on questioning him, he straightened up and said to them, "Let any one of you who is without sin be the first to throw a stone at her." Again he stooped down and wrote on the ground.

At this, those who heard began to go away one at a time, the older ones first, until only Jesus was left, with the woman still standing there. Jesus straightened up and asked her, "Woman, where are they? Has no one condemned you?"

"No one, sir," she said.

"Then neither do I condemn you," Jesus declared. "Go now and leave your life of sin." (John 8:1–11)

Half-clothed and exposed before a tribunal of angry men, the woman was thrust before Jesus. She has done wrong, there's no doubt about that. Perhaps she was set up. Where was the man in this tryst? How did he escape so easily? The woman was easy to capture, easy to drag through the streets by her hair. But it wasn't justice that these men wanted. It was entrapment of Jesus that they were after. One wrong word from him could break the trust he had with his radical and uneducated band of followers.

We don't know what Jesus wrote in the sand that day. In fact, this is the only record we have of Jesus writing anything. Wouldn't you love to know what it was? But perhaps it isn't really that important. Perhaps he bent down to write in the sand so that the attention would be removed, momentarily, from the humiliated woman. When Jesus was pressed for an answer again and again, he finally said the words that pierced even the hardest of hearts. *"Let any one of you who is without sin be the first to throw a stone at her."*

When at last the crowd of accusers drifted away, dropping their stones as they exited the scene, only then did Jesus address the woman: *"Neither do I condemn you."*

It's not that Jesus accepted her sin. In fact, he instructed her very clearly to stop doing what she was doing, to change her ways. Jesus is never tolerant of wrong behavior. But he revealed love by giving her a new way of life.

At some time we have probably all seen a television show or movie that portrays a courtroom, complete with judge, jury and attorneys. We watch the dramatic exchanges with keen interest, wondering what the final verdict will be. Depending on our point of view, we silently cheer for the side we want to win. The sentencing brings closure and relief, and the court is finally adjourned.

This incident with the adulterous woman is a picture of what we can understand about our own personal "courtroom." In our minds, we often see ourselves in a similar situation. We see ourselves as being on trial for the crime of being human, with failings and weaknesses and even sins. The judge is God himself, the jury is our family and friends, and our lawyer is...wait a minute! Who is our lawyer?

In the shows, there is always a prosecuting attorney and a defense attorney. The prosecutor does his best to assure the guilt of the person on trial. He blames and accuses with vehemence, declaring that every motive is so unquestionably evil that there is no doubt of guilt. The defense attorney, on the other hand, works tirelessly to prove the innocence of the defendant. He counters every argument with an explanation that shows another side to the story. He not only wants to deny the accusations of the prosecutor, he strives to dismiss the accusations altogether. *"But if anybody does sin, we have one who speaks to the Father in our defense—Jesus Christ, the Righteous One"* (1 John 2:1).

This scripture tells us that Jesus is, in fact, your defense attorney—your advocate, the one who pleads your case. He is the one who sits by you while you stand trial, and he guarantees that you will be proclaimed innocent. He is on your side and will protect you because you have claimed him for your own. You have "attorney/client" privilege.

Your perspective of the courtroom of life makes all the difference. Jesus is not your accuser and he never has been. That's Satan's job, and he does it quite well, we can assure you. But when Jesus rises to take his stand, the judge listens. Every single thing that you are accused of is wiped away. The verdict is more than "not guilty"; in fact, in the judge's view, because of Jesus, you are now found innocent, righteous and even perfect! All charges are dismissed.

> **RANDY:** *I love having the right people on my side! Don't you? As a kid playing touch football after school, it was always great to get the really hot players on my team. In high school it was nice having as great friends the super athlete in the school and the super-brain senior class president. I like it when my wife is on my side of a disagreement. I like it when my grandkids are on my team (they think I'm smart, strong and can do anything. Shhh...don't tell them the truth!). And when I figured out that my defender is Jesus and my defender's dad is the judge and that I am actually my defender's younger brother, which means that the judge is also my dad, I felt very, very confident of the outcome of the trial. Especially with my older brother Jesus being willing to take on any punishment I might deserve. Like I said, I love having the right people on my side!*

Does this give you the liberty to commit more crimes? Of course not. On the contrary, this verdict is the inspiration to live up to the innocence that has been attributed to you!

Jesus revealed love to the woman caught in adultery, and his reaction to her situation reveals love to us over 2,000 years later.

A Love-Revealing Rescue

We all love stories about daring rescues. Our heroes are those who find ways to save the lives of those in trouble. When we think of the firefighters during the 9/11 attacks, we remember how they rushed up the stairs in an effort to rescue the perishing. When we hear of medical teams or military units urgently responding to a call for help, we're filled with admiration for their dedication. Often, the rescuers risk their own lives in order to save the life of another.

Of course, the whole of Jesus' life was a rescue mission. He came to live on this earth in order to save those who would believe in him. He offers eternal life, forgiveness, freedom from sin and guilt, and the joy of knowing God. He rescues us from our sin and from ourselves! He reshapes lives and relationships. He is a hero!

But he also rescued a drowning fisherman one night on the Sea of Galilee. Jesus had stayed on land to dismiss the crowds and to take some time for prayer while his disciples were instructed to take the boat and head to the other side of the lake. As the night went on, the winds began to blow and the boat began to sway. Before the night ended, the disciples would see a hero in action.

> Shortly before dawn Jesus went out to them, walking on the lake. When the disciples saw him walking on the lake, they were terrified. "It's a ghost," they said, and cried out in fear.
>
> But Jesus immediately said to them: "Take courage! It is I. Don't be afraid."
>
> "Lord, if it's you," Peter replied, "tell me to come to you on the water."
>
> "Come," he said.
>
> Then Peter got down out of the boat, walked on the water and came toward Jesus. But when he saw the wind, he was afraid and, beginning to sink, cried out, "Lord, save me!"
>
> Immediately Jesus reached out his hand and caught him. "You of little faith," he said, "why did you doubt?"
>
> And when they climbed into the boat, the wind died down. Then those who were in the boat worshiped him, saying, "Truly you are the Son of God." (Matthew 14:25–33)

Please remember that these are grown men who are accustomed to seeing lots of activity on the sea, and yet they'd never seen anything like this. As they followed Jesus, they had seen disease and demons, so they were not feeble or easily frightened. Yet the sight of a figure on the water was enough to make them cry like children.

We have to point out that this happens in our day and age, although maybe not quite so literally. Grown men and women who are confronted with the real Jesus sometimes don't recognize him. Assumptions made throughout life present Jesus as a soft and safe life preserver, but when he appears in his real form, there is often an instant reaction of fear. He startled and shocked the fishermen, and he does the same today.

The scripture says that Jesus "immediately" reassured them. He was quick to lessen their anxiety. His love found no pleasure in allowing them to experience unnecessary terror. But Peter, in one of his many impulsive moments of risk-taking, wanted to make sure. Instead of inviting Jesus to come aboard, he asked Jesus for permission to come to him on the water.

"Come," said Jesus. Now, walking on water was not something Jesus had asked Peter to do. It wasn't a command for the apostles; it wasn't taught to his followers. But at this time, Jesus told Peter to come to him. If Jesus told Peter that he could do it, then Peter could. And Peter did!

Until...the wind and the waves distracted him from Jesus, and he began to sink. The best part about this time in the life of Peter is what he did when he started going down: *"Lord, save me!"* Peter knew whom to call on in a time of trouble. Immediately—there's that word again—Jesus reached out his hand and caught him. Jesus is the rescuer, the first responder, the hero. He saved Peter from drowning in those billowing waves.

Even before they made it back to the boat, Jesus asked Peter why he doubted. Simple question, simple answer: "Waves! Water!" What answer would you have given, if you were Peter? Maybe something like: "I was afraid; it made no sense, and I didn't want to do it anymore!" Interestingly, those are the same answers we seem to give to Jesus whenever we back out of doing what he calls us to do!

But maybe Peter's problem was not only about doubting Jesus, but about doubting himself. He seemed to believe Jesus could walk on water; he even believed Jesus could save him from drowning. But he doubted that he could do something that Jesus absolutely said he could. He started to see himself through his own eyes instead of through the eyes of Jesus. He focused on the waves and what he couldn't do, instead of what Jesus said he could do.

Jesus did not rebuke Peter for trying. He did not rebuke Peter for stepping out of the boat. His love for Peter is evidenced by the fact that he immediately reached out and rescued him from the water and also from his doubts. And when they got back in the boat and the disciples worshipped, who do you think worshipped the most? Now, not only did he believe who Jesus was, he believed that Jesus would not let him down. Even Peter's doubts did not stop Jesus' rescuing love!

A Love-Revealing Touch

Jesus healed many times throughout his ministry, and it's interesting to note the number of women that he brought to health. At a time when women were marginalized, Jesus saw them through the eyes of love and compassion. One woman in particular was given special treatment by Jesus.

> On a Sabbath Jesus was teaching in one of the synagogues, and a woman was there who had been crippled by a spirit for eighteen years. She was bent over and could not straighten up at all. When Jesus saw her, he called her forward and said to her, "Woman, you are set free from your infirmity." Then he put his hands on her, and immediately she straightened up and praised God.
>
> Indignant because Jesus had healed on the Sabbath, the synagogue leader said to the people, "There are six days for work. So come and be healed on those days, not on the Sabbath."
>
> The Lord answered him, "You hypocrites! Doesn't each of you on the Sabbath untie your ox or donkey from the stall and lead it out to give it water? Then should not this woman, a daughter of Abraham, whom Satan has kept bound for eighteen long years, be set free on the Sabbath day from what bound her?" (Luke 13:10–16)

This woman had been staring at the ground for eighteen years. In spite of her severe handicap, where do we find her on the Sabbath? She was in the synagogue, where she would have the opportunity to hear the Word of God, even if she had to listen with her face in the dust. In his love, Jesus saw her as someone who was bound by Satan, suffering from a great infirmity. His healing touch caused her to stand up for the first time in what must have seemed like forever. And her response to this healing was to praise God.

When the complainers made their case against the healing, the loving Jesus revealed his indignation with their lack of compassion. His comparison to the care of animals is not at all meant to be demeaning to her; in fact he is making a strong point in contrast. If the animals can be helped on a Sabbath day, how much more should this woman receive healing? Then Jesus gave her a title that is more honorable than any other for a woman of that time: *"daughter of Abraham."* Abraham, the father of the Jewish faith, was held in the highest regard for the Hebrew nation. Nowhere else in the Scriptures is any woman given this honor.

Jesus' love-revealing touch did not just heal the woman. He gave her dignity and worth. That's what love does.

A Love-Revealing Death

Jesus lived his life to reveal love. But that life would have been incomplete if he had not accepted the death that he had to face. Jesus knew from the beginning that he would have to die. He tried to explain it to his disciples again and again, but they had a hard time understanding it. Perhaps we do, too. None of us fully understand what it took for Jesus to go to the cross. We don't completely comprehend all the reasons that the plan of salvation included his substitutionary death. But we know, by faith, that without that death we would still be controlled and consumed by sin. We now have the freedom and power that he provided because he went to the cross.

> *But we do see Jesus, who was made lower than the angels for a little while, now crowned with glory and honor because he suffered death, so that by the grace of God he might taste death for everyone....*
>
> *Since the children have flesh and blood, he too shared in their humanity so that by his death he might break the power of him who holds the power of death—that is, the devil—and free those who all their lives were held in slavery by their fear of death. (Hebrews 2:9, 14–15)*

We admit that all of us wrestle with the fear of dying. We don't want to suffer unnecessary pain. That is normal and necessary for survival. But there's a difference between a fear of dying and a fear of death. Because of Jesus, death is no longer an unknown journey into a dark abyss. Jesus has gone through it, and has arisen victorious! And because we believe in him and follow him, we can face death with the same victory. Jesus revealed love because he tasted death for you and for me.

Jesus Reveals Radical Love

And I pray that you, being rooted and established in love, may have power, together with all the Lord's holy people, to grasp how wide and long and high and deep is the love of Christ, and to know this love that surpasses knowledge—that you may be filled to the measure of all the fullness of God. (Ephesians 3:17–19)

The love of Jesus is so radical that we will never understand it perfectly. The knowledge of this love *"surpasses knowledge."* We are finite creatures and Jesus' love is infinite. Although it's beyond us, we must dedicate our lives to discovering it again and again. There is no greater or loftier goal than discovering the love of Jesus. The more we know of it, the more we want to give it away, to share it, to let it flow from our lives into the lives of others. It is Jesus, our Savior, who reveals, in flesh and blood, the very essence of RADICAL LOVE.

HE IS MY SAVIOR

Unknown author/Adapted

He came from the bosom of the Father to the bosom of woman. He put on humanity that we might put on divinity. He became the Son of Man that we might become the sons of God. He came from Heaven where flowers never fade, rivers never freeze and frosts never chill the air. There are no undertakers and no graveyards, for no one ever dies, nor is anyone ever buried.

He was born contrary to the laws of nature, reared in obscurity, and lived in poverty. Only once did he cross the boundary of his homeland, in childhood. He had no wealth or influence, had neither training nor formal education. His relatives were inconspicuous and uninfluential.

In infancy he started a King; in boyhood he puzzled the doctors; in manhood he ruled the course of nature. He walked upon the billows, hushed the sea to sleep, and healed the multitudes without medicine.

He never wrote a book, yet not all the libraries of the country could hold the books that have been written about him. He never wrote a song, but he has furnished the theme for more songs than all songwriters combined. He never marshalled an army, drafted a soldier, or fired a gun, yet no leader ever made more volunteers. He is the star of astronomy, the rock of geology, and the lion and lamb of zoology. Great men have come and gone, yet he lives on. Herod could not kill him, Satan could not seduce him, death could not destroy him, and the grave could not hold him.

He laid aside his purple robe for a peasant's garb. He was rich, yet for our sakes he became poor. He slept in another's manger, he cruised the lake in another's boat. He rode on another's beast, and he was buried in another's tomb. All men have failed; he never failed. He is the ever-perfect one. He is the chief among ten thousand and is altogether lovely. He is the revelation of love—HE IS MY SAVIOR!

PART THREE

SECRETS OF LOVE

LOVE SECRET 1

Destroying Love

Truth is not always an easy thing to handle. Jesus stated the words, "I tell you the truth" over eighty times in the Bible. In fact, telling the truth got him killed. Jesus embodied truth. Jesus lived truth. Jesus taught truth. Jesus was THE truth. Telling the truth was the only thing he could do. Jesus said that the truth would set us free. It sets us free from the guilt of sin, sets us free from the power of sin, sets us free from the condemnation of sin and sets us free to love! *"To the Jews who had believed him, Jesus said, 'If you hold to my teaching, you are really my disciples. Then you will know the truth, and the truth will set you free'"* (John 8:31–32).

The first love secret is very straightforward: destroying our capacity to love occurs because of sin. When sin gets into the equation of any relationship, it becomes a destroyer. You lose when you sin; you lose what's most important in life. Love is what we know to be supreme in life, and so love must be protected. To do this we need to understand that to the degree we embrace sin, to that same degree we destroy our capacity to love. It's like having a cup filled up with water. Once it's filled, you can't put any more in. You would have to pour some of the old out to put something new in. If our lives (cups) are filled up with sin, there is no room for love. As we empty out our lives from sin, we can fill up our lives with love.

Sin Destroys Our Capacity to Love

At the beginning of this book we were reminded that God is love. Since we were created in his image, we were given the capacity to love. If anyone (Christian or pseudo-Christian or non-Christian) puts into practice what God says love is, they will experience love to some extent. Truth is still truth, and it will work for anyone in any place. But it is only the true Christian who intimately knows God and who strives to live the life of love that experiences the degree of love humans were meant to have. It is only the Christian who has been given the Spirit of God to live inside him. One component of the fruit of the Spirit is love, and so it is only the spirit-filled Christian who is empowered by God to love. Jesus defined love for all time when he died on the cross for all mankind. Therefore, a Christian's response to God's love is what ultimately allows a person to be filled with love.

This is how God showed his love among us: He sent his one and only Son into the world that we might live through him. This is love: not that we loved God, but that he loved us and sent his Son as an atoning sacrifice for our sins. (1 John 4:9–10)

We love because he first loved us. (1 John 4:19)

Dear friends, let us love one another, for love comes from God. Everyone who loves has been born of God and knows God. Whoever does not love does not know God, because God is love. (1 John 4:7–8)

As we delve into the effects of sin on a person's life, we want to remind the Christian who has been forgiven of their sins that:

You are not your past.
You are not your mistakes.
You are not your parents.
You are not your pain.
You are not your addiction.
You are not your failures.
You are not your sin.

You are God's beloved.
You are wonderfully made.
You are forgiven.
You are God's son.
You are God's daughter.

> You are accepted.
> You are cleansed.
> You are a new creation!
> *Unknown author/Adapted*

Now let's take a closer look at sin. Sin is not a popular topic. It's not going to be on the bestseller list. If you want to disperse a crowd, talk about sin! The word used for sin in the Greek language was an archery term and it literally meant "to miss the mark." When a person tried to hit the bull's eye with an arrow but missed, it would be called a sin...it missed the mark of the perfect shot. When we take aim at life and miss the perfect life we were created to live, we sin. We miss the mark. But sin is even more than that. Sin is failure. Sin is missing life. Sin is breaking the law of God. Sin is breaking the heart of God.

WHAT IS SIN?

Unknown author/Adapted

Man calls it an accident; God calls it an abomination.
Man calls it a blunder; God calls it a blindness.
Man calls it a defect; God calls it a disaster.
Man calls it a chance; God calls it a choice.
Man calls it an error; God calls it an enmity.
Man calls it a fascination; God calls it a fatality.
Man calls it an infirmity; God calls in an iniquity.
Man calls it a luxury; God calls it a leprosy.
Man calls it a liberty; God calls it a liability.
Man calls it a trifle; God calls it a tragedy.
Man calls it weakness; God calls it willfulness.
Man calls it a mistake; God calls it a madness.

The first time we were confronted with the following scriptures we did not especially like it. It revealed so much that was so wrong in our lives. And it was so definitive...that those who live like this will not go to heaven.

The acts of the flesh are obvious: sexual immorality, impurity and debauchery; idolatry and witchcraft; hatred, discord, jealousy, fits of rage, selfish ambition, dissensions, factions and envy; drunkenness, orgies, and the like. I warn you, as I did before, that those who live like this will not inherit the kingdom of God. (Galatians 5:19–21)

...for all have sinned and fall short of the glory of God. (Romans 3:23)

If anyone, then, knows the good they ought to do and doesn't do it, it is sin for them. (James 4:17)

Some sin is blatant; it is easily seen. Some sin is latent; it's a little more hidden. The sin you can't see can be the most deadly. Sin includes doing the wrong things as well as not doing the right things. Sometimes people don't want to see themselves as sinners, but in order to understand how to love, we must be aware of what sin does in our lives.

RANDY: *At the age of seventeen, I called myself a Christian, although I was beginning to see the inconsistences between the life I was living and the way Christianity was described in the Bible. Because of false teaching and mistaken beliefs, I had not taken sin seriously. I realized that I had cheapened God's grace and had never truly become a Christian. I felt saved, but I had believed a lie. It's like the woman in NYC that I heard about. She, a court stenographer, had been called out of court during a trial and gently told by a clerk that they had received a phone call from her cousin to tell her that her father had died. This news was devastating. She tried to call home but only got an answering machine with her dad's voice on it. This caused her to break down in tears. Later she was finally able to connect with her cousin to ask how her father had died. She found out it was not her dad who had died but her cousin's dad who had died. So, in the end, it was her uncle who had passed away. Yet for hours this misled woman felt exactly the way she would feel if her father had really died. The pain, the heartache, the grief...those were true feelings even though they were based on wrong information. Our feelings affect* *our nervous system the same as facts do. So, we can be deceived by our feelings. For me, I felt saved for years but I was misled. My feelings were wrong. When I understood from a Bible study on a Monday night on September 24, 1973 that I was still a sinner separated from God because I had never come to God on his terms, I got urgent. I was baptized into Christ that night, making Jesus the Lord of my life and getting my sins washed away. At that point I not only felt saved, I was saved! There's a memorable line from a sermon that I heard many years ago that speaks to my situation and to many other people's situations too. It goes like this: "When a sincerely wrong person is confronted with the truth, he either ceases to be sincere or he ceases to be wrong."*

KAY: Although I had been raised with a lot of Bible teaching, the concept of sin seemed "old-fashioned" to me. During my teenage and college years in the 1970s, my goal was to find myself through any means possible, even by behavior that I had always been taught was wrong. I considered myself smarter and more sensible by living my life my own way. I wasn't about to let anyone tell me what to do. But to please my friends, I was reading the Bible from time to time. When I read one of the passages in the Scriptures that lists sins (Galatians 5:19–21), I became indignant. Now it was this book telling me what I didn't want to hear! I slammed the Bible down on my bedside table, resolved to never pick it up again. But I did pick it up again later, and continued to read. One day a friend sat me down to talk about my life. I was still defensive. "Why should I become a Christian?" I asked. She had an open Bible in her lap and she hit it with her hand. "Because YOU are a SINNER," she exclaimed, with great passion! For once, I didn't react. I nodded my head and sheepishly agreed. It wasn't too long after that day that I repented of my sins and was baptized into Christ on August 18, 1974.

To live in sin is to be spiritually lost. What does it mean to be lost? It means being without direction in life—not knowing your purpose, not knowing your reason for existing, not knowing where you're going. It means feeling guilty because you are guilty. It means being scared. It means being insecure. It means being lonely even in a crowd. It means having superficial relationships. It means allowing the hurts and pains, the scars of the past and the disappointments of the past to leave you negative, in despair and hopeless. Often in our lost state it feels like nobody understands, that nobody really cares, that nobody needs us. It can feel like you don't belong. It can feel like you are of no value to anyone. It can feel like you are meaningless. Again, we know this to be true because of personal experience and because God says it's true: *"Wickedness overthrows the sinner"* (Proverbs 13:6). *"Trouble pursues the sinner"* (Proverbs 13:21). *"In the paths of the wicked are snares and pitfalls"* (Proverbs 22:5).

It is further stated in Romans 6:23 that the wages of sin is death. If a person chooses to work at a job or a profession, the person would expect to be paid for the work that has been done. That person would have earned their wages. In the same way, if a person chooses to sin, then what they have earned for themselves is death. The symptoms of death are already at work right now. Sin brings death to relationships, which in turn brings death to love. There are too many people in this world to even try to count who are experiencing their love slowly dying. It may be love in a marriage that is dying. Or it may be love in a family that is dying. Or it may be self-love that is dying. According to Isaiah 59:1–2, sin separates:

> *Surely the arm of the Lord is not too short to save,*
> *   nor his ear too dull to hear.*
> *But your iniquities have separated*
> *   you from your God;*
> *your sins have hidden his face from you,*
> *   so that he will not hear.*

Sin affects your life before becoming a Christian. Sin affects your life after becoming a Christian. If you take sin lightly, it takes you seriously. Sin is no respecter of persons. Sin will destroy anyone. When you are sick, you go to the doctor. The doctor says, "Tell me your symptoms and I'll tell you your problem." When he tells you how to get well, you don't argue with the doctor. Jesus is the Great Physician. He tells us that all problems in life have one root problem...the root problem being sin. Now, don't argue with the doctor! Sin kills love. Sin kills relationships. Sin separates you from God. Sin separates you from yourself. Sin separates you from others you want to be close to.

Sin Separates from God

Let's read the story of David's sin with Bathsheba.

In the spring, at the time when kings go off to war, David sent Joab out with the king's men and the whole Israelite army. They destroyed the Ammonites and besieged Rabbah. But David remained in Jerusalem.

One evening David got up from his bed and walked around on the roof of the palace. From the roof he saw a woman bathing. The woman was very beautiful, and David sent someone to find out about her. The man said, "She is Bathsheba, the daughter of Eliam and the wife of Uriah the Hittite." Then David sent messengers to get her. She came to him, and he slept with her. (Now she was purifying herself from her monthly uncleanness.) Then she went back home. The woman conceived and sent word to David, saying, "I am pregnant."

So David sent this word to Joab: "Send me Uriah the Hittite." And Joab sent him to David. When Uriah came to him, David asked him how Joab was, how the soldiers were and how the war was going. Then David said to Uriah, "Go down to your house and wash your feet." So Uriah left the palace, and a gift from the king was sent after him. But Uriah slept at the entrance to the palace with all his master's servants and did not go down to his house.

David was told, "Uriah did not go home." So he asked Uriah, "Haven't you just come from a military campaign? Why didn't you go home?"

Uriah said to David, "The ark and Israel and Judah are staying in tents, and my commander Joab and my lord's men are camped in the open country. How could I go to my house to eat and drink and make love to my wife? As surely as you live, I will not do such a thing!"

Then David said to him, "Stay here one more day, and tomorrow I will send you back." So Uriah remained in Jerusalem that day and the next. At David's invitation, he ate and drank with him, and David made him drunk. But in the evening Uriah went out to sleep on his mat among his master's servants; he did not go home.

In the morning David wrote a letter to Joab and sent it with Uriah. In it he wrote, "Put Uriah out in front where the fighting is fiercest. Then withdraw from him so he will be struck down and die."...

When Uriah's wife heard that her husband was dead, she mourned for him. After the time of mourning was over, David had her brought to his house, and she became his wife and bore him a son. But the thing David had done displeased the LORD. (2 Samuel 11:1–15, 26–27)

David was lazy. David was lustful. David committed adultery. David lied. David committed murder. And this did not seem to displease society. In fact, most sin does not displease society. But it did displease God! David hid his problem for many months. Perhaps his attitude was that if no one could see it, then no one would know about it. "After all," he might have reasoned, "everyone does it; therefore who really cares about it?" He had forgotten that God cares and that God knows.

We may think our sin is hidden, but our lives will show God's displeasure. God gives life. God also withholds life. God is not passive about sin. In fact, God bears down. Portions of David's Psalm 38 expose what can happen as a result of a person's sin:

1. Feeling down and depressed: *Your arrows have pierced me, and your hand has come down on me...all day long I go about mourning...I am feeble and utterly crushed; I groan in anguish of heart.*

2. Having health issues (Note: Not all health issues are a result of sin! Scripture makes that abundantly clear through people like Job or the man born blind.): *Because of your wrath there is no health in my body; there is no soundness in my bones because of my sin....My*

> back is filled with searing pain; there is no health in my body.

3. Feeling guilty: *My guilt has overwhelmed me like a burden too heavy to bear.*

4. Having high stress and high blood pressure: *My heart pounds, my strength fails me.*

5. Feeling unhappy and hopeless: *Even the light has gone from my eyes.*

6. Becoming paranoid, thinking people are out to get you or talking about you behind your back: *My friends and companions avoid me because of my wounds; my neighbors stay far away. Those who want to kill me set their traps, those who would harm me talk of my ruin; all day long they scheme and lie.*

7. Being quiet and inactive when dealing with sin and righteousness: *I am like the deaf, who cannot hear, like the mute, who cannot speak; I have become like one who does not hear, whose mouth can offer no reply.*

So whether you believe it or not, you feel pressure. You will not perform as well in life. You can't be all you want to be because the guilt is real. So, sin is serious. Sin wipes you out. And it is sin that separates a person from God.

Sin Separates from Self

Sin separates us from who God intended us to be. Why do people sin? People get deceived. In Psalm 73, Asaph expresses how he got deceived by those who were living worldly lives. He started thinking everything went their way, their life was easy, they were rich and getting richer and life was just better for them somehow. He started thinking that what the world had to offer was more satisfying than what God had to offer. He got to the point in his thinking that trying to be righteous was getting him nowhere in life. He even found himself unmotivated to get up in the morning.

For I envied the arrogant
*   when I saw the prosperity of the wicked.*
They have no struggles;
*   their bodies are healthy and strong.*
They are free from common human burdens;
*   they are not plagued by human ills....*

This is what the wicked are like—
*   always free of care, they go on amassing wealth.*
Surely in vain I have kept my heart pure
*   and have washed my hands in innocence.*
All day long I have been afflicted,
*   and every morning brings new punishments.*

Asaph finally pulled it all together but not without a battle to finally get the right spiritual and right eternal perspective. Another way to get deceived by sin is by believing that through a sinful behavior you will "find yourself" or find the most happiness. There's no denying that some sin brings pleasure. But it is short-lived pleasure. Moses knew this. He chose to be *"mistreated along with the people of God rather than to enjoy the fleeting pleasures of sin"* (Hebrews 11:25). The external beauty of sin is painted for us by Satan, but he hides the pictures of what sin ultimately produces in people's lives. He hides the pictures of the tears of broken marriages and broken families. Satan does not want us to see the faces of the children who are unloved or unwanted. We are not shown the dead bodies from drunk drivers or the pain of the families at the funerals. Nor do we see the pictures of the multitude of aborted children. In the Old Testament we find passages that speak of children being sacrificed to heathen gods. People think this is horrible, brutal and barbaric. Yet now children are sacrificed to the god of self as they are killed in clean, sterilized rooms with procedures done by highly educated professionals. Precious infants are regarded as a nuisance and a problem to be destroyed. More than a billion and a half abortions have been performed worldwide in the last 40 years. 55 million were aborted last year alone. That's 115,000 per day. In the United States there were over a million abortions last year. 20% were by teenagers; 32% were by 20–24 year olds. Statistics show that 43% of all women in the US will have an abortion by the time they are 45 years old.

"Hey, King David, how long was that pleasure with Bathsheba? Thirty minutes? An hour?" We can tell you that the pain lasts a lot longer! Although Satan strives to paint an illusion about sin, it is really a delusion.

There is an old *Twilight Zone* television episode that portrays this pretty well. In the story, creatures came from outer space to the earth and began to stop human illness and hunger. They offered to take earthlings back to their planet, where they would live lives without disease or poverty. During their recruitment of the earthlings, one scientist found one of their books and began to translate it. At first, he could only figure out how to translate the title. It read: *How to Serve Man.* The people on earth were delighted that these visitors had come to help and serve mankind. But as many humans were embarking on their spacecraft to go with the aliens, the scientist translated more of the book. In the final scene, he is seen running toward the spaceship, waving his arms and screaming for people not to get on board. You see, he had figured out that the book *How to Serve Man* was really a cookbook! The earthlings were being transported to the aliens' planet to be eaten!

What seemed so good was all just one big lie. They were being deceived.

If you had asked David after his tryst with Bathsheba, "How are you doing, David?" he might have replied: "I feel pretty good about myself." For months he lied to himself about the gravity of his sin. He hid his sin and tried to feel good about what he had done. But sin is like a Pandora's Box. When you want to close it, you can't. Life becomes trying to feel good about yourself. Life becomes trying to get people to like you and respect you. Life becomes trying to keep others from really knowing you.

Sin—first appealing, then appalling
Sin—first enticing, then enslaving
Sin—first alluring, then alienating
Sin—promises life, produces death
Sin is the most disappointing thing in all the world.

Sin causes a person to lose their self-respect. They know they are hiding. They know they are settling for second best. They know they are letting go of their dreams and ideals. Their sin may be an Internet pornography addiction or a gaming addiction. It may be alcohol or drug abuse. It may be having premarital or extramarital sex in order to feel loved or wanted or needed. It may be anger problems. Wrong choices and a wrong focus can cause low self-esteem. This can lead to having an unhealthy concern about your appearance and an obsession with your body image, causing eating disorders. Yes, sin damages big-time!

One thing is for sure about sin: it will be found out. No one gets away with anything. There are always consequences both in this life and in the next. 1 Timothy 5:24 tells us: *"The sins of some men are obvious, reaching the place of judgment ahead of them; the sins of others trail behind them."* As time goes on and a person does not deal with and take responsibility for their sin, it becomes easier and easier to say, "Just one more time." Our hearts become hardened and our consciences become desensitized. There is a continual lust for more because you can never get enough of any sin to be satisfied and content. Sin never leaves us with the fulfillment we crave and need.

In Psalm 51, David says, *"My sin is always before me."* In other words, he couldn't shake the guilt. He was always thinking about it. He lost sleep thinking about it. Like Esau, who sold his birthright to satisfy his immediate desire and lust, David couldn't take his sin back. The deed was done. That's the way sin is. The deeper in sin we get, the deeper in sin we are enticed to go. It can even lead to such a hopelessness and dislike of ourselves that we might think to destroy ourselves. A person can become so separated from themselves by their sin that the thought or action of suicide becomes a reality. In the US, one out of every five teens has contemplated suicide. That's 20% of all teenagers in America. Amazing! Sin can leave a person feeling worthless. Sin can leave us hurting emotionally to such a degree that it leads to cutting, burning, drinking or taking drugs. Four out of ten teens (40%) in the US have afflicted self-injury. There are three million teens presently suffering from alcoholism, and three out of ten teen girls will become pregnant before the age of twenty in the US. One out of ten teens has been raped. Sin starts early and the effects of sin can last a lifetime. Sin can even destroy to the extent where people will harm and kill others before destroying themselves. The number of stabbings and shootings are on the rise at an alarming rate.

So sin separates us from God. And sin separates us from ourselves. But sin is not done with us yet!

Sin Separates from Others

Sin separates us from others. It can even separate us from those we wish to love the most. Sin does not get us to pay attention to how we are hurting others. We don't ask, "Why the tears?" or "Why the frustration?" People become self-centered and indifferent. They don't let others get too close, out of fear of discovery. They don't ask: "How does my coldness affect you?" or "How does my lying affect you?" or "How does my anger affect you?" They tend to become harsh with others.

Again, take David as our example. When the prophet, Nathan, confronted David about his sin he told him a story. He told of a man who owned one special lamb that he loved very much. But another man, who had many lambs, selfishly took the one special lamb. When David heard this story, his reaction was quite harsh. He declared that the selfish man should die! Although the law specified that in this type of situation the lamb should be replaced with four lambs, David's judgment was severe. Because of the sin in his own life, he had no grace for the sin of others. This is typical when we aren't dealing with sin in our lives. The tendency is to be very critical of others, to resist close relationships and to confess very little. Sin pushes people away and destroys the potential for love.

When sin is involved, a very fine line exists between hate and love. David's son Amnon was in love (maybe more in lust) with Tamar his half-sister. He devised a plan to be with her, and then forced himself upon her. He ended up raping her. After this, he hated her. *"Then Amnon hated her with intense hatred. In fact, he hated her more than he had loved her. Amnon said to her, "Get up and get out!"* (2 Samuel 13:15).

Yes, it's a thin line that gets too easily crossed. About 40% of the women who get killed worldwide are attacked by a current or former husband, a cohabiting partner, a date or a boyfriend. Just in the

United States alone, three women are murdered by their husbands or boyfriends every day. Sexual infidelity drives both men and women into rage, hatred, jealousy and even murder. Sexual sins affect people at their deepest emotional levels. So many just want to love and be loved and they can't figure out what gets in the way. It's always sin that gets in the way. It's always a sin problem that separates people. The divorce rate around the world is staggering.

TOP 10 DIVORCE RATES BY COUNTRY

10. United States—53%
9. France—55%
8. Cuba—56%
7. Estonia—58%
6. Luxembourg—60%
5. Spain—61%
4. Czech Republic—66%
3. Hungary—67%
2. Portugal—68%
1. Belgium—71%

But these statistics don't include all the breakups from all who cohabit but don't marry. People who claim an undying love fall waste to the pain and heartache of failed love. The children often become the battleground for resentments and revenge, and so the tragedy only worsens. Families are torn apart and stop talking to each other because of the sin that never gets forgiven or resolved. Abused kids often grow up to find themselves becoming the verbal, physical or sexual abusers. They become the very thing they once despised.

So sin damages and sin destroys. Sin separates us from God. Sin separates us from ourselves. And sin separates us from others as love is smashed and demolished. Our sin is too heavy a burden for us to bear. The great news is that we can be forgiven. Our lives can be changed. We can live the lives we were created to live!

You see, at just the right time, when we were still power-less, Christ died for the ungodly. Very rarely will anyone die for a righteous person, though for a good person someone might possibly dare to die. But God demonstrates his own love for us in this: While we were still sinners, Christ died for us. (Romans 5:6–8)

As we close out **Love Secret 1,** let us share this story with you:

There was once a farmer who had a son and he wanted him to learn about God's forgiveness. Every time the young boy would do something wrong, the father would give the son a large nail and send him to pound it half way into the barn door. After a few years there were numerous nails in the barn door. One day, the father called the son into the kitchen to talk. He told him of God's love for him and about Jesus dying on the cross for the forgiveness of his sins. He told the son to take the hammer and go pull out all the nails from the barn door. When the boy returned, the father took all the nails and threw them in the trash explaining that because of Jesus, God is not counting (1, 2, 3, etc.) our sins against us. But the son asked the question, "But what about all the nail holes left in the barn door?" The father gently said, "God can forgive us of all our sins, but the scars of our sin are still there."

God forgives, but we have to live with our scars from the sins we've committed or from the sins that have been committed against us. The earlier in life a person becomes a disciple of Jesus and chooses to no longer embrace and accept a life of sin, the fewer scars are in their lives. We see too many people having the attitude of wanting to "live it up" with sin now and become a Christian later. This shows not only the total lack of understanding and disregard of God's love and sacrifice through Jesus, but it also shows the incredible naivety about the destruction that sin leaves in its wake.

RANDY: I have scars all over my body. I have one on my leg from falling off a skateboard. I have one from hitting a rusted drum with my foot while treading water in a lake. I have one on my wrist from a nail sticking out in a storage crawl space. I have one from an appendix operation. I have one from knee surgery. I have one on my ankle from a piece of sharp metal. And I have a scar on my chest more than a foot long from two operations for cancer. I remember where I got each scar and how I got each scar and when I got each scar. All these places where my flesh was gashed or sliced open have healed, but the scars will remain there for all my life. And that's how it is with the scars in our lives from the sins we have committed or from the sins that have been committed by others against us. At times I have to emotionally deal with my scars from past hurts, disappointments or failures. But I am always forgiven. I always have Jesus who comforts and sympathizes. I always have my new life. I don't have to be defined any longer by my scars! I no longer have to be negative, in despair or hopeless. Amazingly enough, the two scars from my cancer saved my life both physically and spiritually. It was those scars that motivated me to search for God. Sometimes it takes some scars in life to get us to see our need for God. And so the scars have become a reminder for me of how horrible and devastating sin is and how wonderful Jesus is that I get to leave my old life behind.

"Come to me, all you who are weary and burdened, and I will give you rest. Take my yoke upon you and learn from me, for I am gentle and humble in heart, and you will find rest for your souls." (Matthew 11:28–29)

When we get our lives right with God, we will get our lives right with ourselves and it will lead to getting our lives right with others. By being connected intimately with God who is love, we will be able to love ourselves and love others in amazing and life-transforming ways. And so Love Secret 1 is...

Sin Destroys Our Capacity to Love

A LIFE'S ROAD
Randy McKean, 1973

As I lay awake in the darkness
With my eyes shut tight to keep the night out,
Knowing that my heart was alone and empty,
I waited for love to fall—
Yet it never would.

When days broke into light
My body was still asleep though I walked
And my mind strove for something;
I searched and found so little,
Knowing life must be more.

Life was leaving my soul
To the point where I wanted to die.
My life was "maybe yes"..."maybe no,"
So I found myself a hope—
She didn't stay long.

I wanted to run; it would make it easy
Just to leave and pretend through life
But my spirit cried, "NO!"
There's more, somewhere there's more—
And so I continued to exist.

I lived, yet I was dying,
For I knew I had no reality—
Oh, I had it all, yet I had nothing, alone in a crowd
And hating each moment more and more—
Lonely, I cried out for life.

Then, almost dead, reality came.
Love was there to see
And life was there to grasp—
I had come to my Crossroads

And there, hope came to my soul.
    A hope of peace.
    A hope of joy.
    A hope of love.
I became real.

LOVE SECRET 2

Forgiving Love

In February 2012, Demetrius Hewlin and two other students were shot and killed in Chardon, Ohio. Soon afterward, Demetrius' mother, Phyllis, told reporters that if she could talk to the shooter, T.J. Lane, she "would tell him I forgive him because, a lot of times, they don't know what they're doing....I taught Demetrius not to live in the past, to live in today, and that forgiveness is divine. You have to forgive everything....Until you've walked in another person's shoes, you don't know what made him come to this point." Lane pleaded guilty to the crime and received a life sentence in prison.

In 2010 Conor McBride lived in Florida and was engaged to marry Ann Grosmaire. But after a quarrel, in a fit of rage, Conor murdered Ann. Her parents, Andy and Kate, felt like their daughter would want them to forgive Conor, which they found nearly impossible to do. In the end, they agreed that Ann, along with Christ, was asking them to forgive. "I had never said no to them," said Andy," so I wasn't going to say no this time. It was just an uplifting of joy and peace." The McBrides visited Conor in prison and later became the cofounders of the Ann Grosmaire "Be the Change" Fund, a charitable fund to promote forgiveness and restorative justice.

In 2014 Claire Davis was a student at Arapahoe High School in Colorado. Walking through the halls at school, she saw a fellow student, eighteen-year-old Karl Pierson, wandering about, heavily armed. "Oh my gosh, Karl," she asked him, "what are you doing?" Karl turned his weapon on Claire and fired, then shot himself. Claire died eight days later. At her memorial service, her father made this statement: "My wife and I forgive Karl Pierson for what he did....We would ask all of you here and all of you watching to search your hearts and also forgive Karl Pierson. He didn't know what he was doing."

In 2006 Charles Roberts walked into an Amish schoolhouse in Pennsylvania and shot eleven young girls. Five of them died. Roberts then turned the gun on himself. The immediate response of the community, including the families of the victims, was to visit Charles Roberts' widow, bringing flowers and food and hugs. At Roberts' funeral, several parents who had just buried their own daughters were in attendance. One father explained, "Our forgiveness was not in our words, it was in what we did."

Members of a Charleston, South Carolina church were gathered for prayer and Bible study one evening in 2015 when a stranger walked in and joined them. After about one hour, the newcomer stood up, raised a gun, and shot nine people. In a court hearing, families of those who were killed expressed forgiveness for the shooter, Dylann Roof. One of those who spoke was Nadine Collier. Her mother, Ethel Lance, was killed in the tragedy. "I just wanted everybody to know, I forgive you," she said. "You took something very precious away from me. I will never get to talk to her ever again. I will never be able to hold her again. But I forgive you, and have mercy on your soul....You hurt me. You hurt a lot of people. If God forgives you, I forgive you."

Every one of these cases of tragedy and forgiveness is shocking. They are shocking in the sense that needless deaths occurred. But they are also shocking because of the forgiveness that was offered by those who suffered. In some ways, it seems unnatural to be able to forgive when something so terrible and hurtful has happened. The need for revenge is so strong in human nature. Yet all the people mentioned above have learned the greatest lesson that can be taught: forgiveness is the key to a life of peace. Forgiveness is crucial to live a life of love.

The "shock" of forgiveness is demonstrated perfectly through Jesus. If only we could really learn the lesson he came to teach! So much of our lives and problems have to do with grudges, resentments, and hurt feelings. What a radical difference it would make if we could really grasp the truth of his message. Marriages, families and nations would be different. Sometimes even within the culture of our churches, our "righteousness" outweighs our mercy. We stand on the rock of truth, but to get there, are we climbing up the pebbles of pettiness?

An incident that portrays these dilemmas and gives great insight into one of love's great secrets is found in Luke 7:36-47:

> *When one of the Pharisees invited Jesus to have dinner with him, he went to the Pharisee's house and reclined at the table. A woman in that town who lived a sinful life learned that Jesus was eating at the Pharisee's house, so she came there with an alabaster jar of perfume. As she stood behind him at his feet weeping, she began to wet his feet with her tears. Then she wiped them with her hair, kissed them and poured perfume on them.*
>
> *When the Pharisee who had invited him saw this, he said to himself, "If this man were a prophet, he would know who is touching him and what kind of woman she is—that she is a sinner."*
>
> *Jesus answered him, "Simon, I have something to tell you."*
>
> *"Tell me, teacher," he said.*
>
> *"Two people owed money to a certain moneylender. One owed him five hundred denarii, and the other fifty. Neither of them had the money to pay him back, so he forgave the debts of both. Now which of them will love him more?"*
>
> *Simon replied, "I suppose the one who had the bigger debt forgiven."*
>
> *"You have judged correctly," Jesus said.*
>
> *Then he turned toward the woman and said to Simon, "Do you see this woman? I came into your house. You did not give me any water for my feet, but she wet my feet with her tears and wiped them with her hair. You did not give me a kiss, but this woman, from the time I entered, has not stopped kissing my feet. You did not put oil on my head, but she has poured perfume on my feet. Therefore, I tell you, her many sins have been forgiven—as her great love has shown. But whoever has been forgiven little loves little."*

Simon the Pharisee was "correct" in his judgment of the woman. Neither the writer (Luke) nor Jesus denied that this woman had lived a sinful life. Simon saw the truth about her. He had a high moral standard, which was not a bad thing in itself. He recognized that certain occupations are unrighteous. No one would say that he should have approved of what she did for a living. In all these things, Simon was obedient to his culture and to God's law. This is important to understand, because we can often quickly dismiss Simon and his perspective. In fact, after Jesus told Simon the story of the debtor and then questioned him about it, Jesus responded: *"You have judged correctly."* So we see that Simon's lifestyle was righteous and his doctrine was spot on. But he was definitely missing something!

The story Jesus told was easy for Simon to understand. If someone cannot pay back money that he owes, then he is extremely grateful if the debt is cancelled. But Simon's problem was that he didn't feel like he owed anyone anything! He certainly didn't think he owed Jesus even the basic hospitality standards. Not only did he consider himself better than the sinful woman, he also considered himself better than Jesus.

Be careful here. There is a temptation we all face when reading this episode to do exactly what Simon did! Oh sure, we don't look down on the woman. But are you looking down on Simon, assuming that you would never do what he did? You see, they are tumultuous waters that we are all being sucked into. It's the strong undertow of self-righteousness. It's a dangerous current, and we must be aware of it in ourselves, even as we see it in Simon the Pharisee!

Love Secret 2 is built on the truth that until we see our own need for forgiveness, we will never be able to love in the way that we should, or could. Pride in ourselves and in our own "goodness" inhibits love for other people, because we will always find something to criticize. But when we understand the vastness of God's forgiveness for us, then we will be able to forgive, and to love, others. To the degree that a person perceives how much forgiveness they need and have been given, to that same degree a person will have the capacity to love and to forgive. This is what Jesus emphasized: whoever has been forgiven little, loves little; whoever has been forgiven much, loves much.

Forgiven Little = Loves Little = Forgives Little
Forgiven Much = Loves Much = Forgives Much

Our purpose in this love secret is not to remind you of all your sins. We don't want you to stop now and make a list of all the things that you have ever done that require forgiveness. That's not a bad exercise, but the point is not how many or how terrible your sins were.

We've even seen instances where people might embellish their sins in order to evoke more feelings of shame. This shows the same misunderstanding that Simon had. Simon assumed that only the "big sins" were the ones that counted. From his perspective, he was living a "better life" than the sinful woman was living. He loved the law and he obeyed it! Let's not forget that. What he needed to realize is that any sin is a "big sin" to God, and any sin is one requiring God's forgiveness.

Forgiveness is never an excuse to approve of wrongdoing. We have already noted that the woman who *"lived a sinful life"* was not excused in her sin. Forgiveness does not mean that we have to approve of a sinful action. In the examples given earlier about tragic murders, we can never accept the taking of a human life. Forgiveness doesn't even mean that a relationship has to be restored. Forgiveness takes the failings of another and lifts those failings into the hands of God, who will do with them as he sees fit. Forgiveness removes our own sense of "fixing" (which could be revenge, bitterness or criticism) and lets God do his work.

Jesus never claimed that forgiveness was easy. If forgiveness were an easy thing, then Jesus would not have had to suffer on the cross the way he did. The cross of Jesus is proof that sin destroys (Love Secret 1). Sin ravages human souls and tears us from God and from one another. Jesus' death on the cross is the evidence that sin is rampant in this world and that sin causes destruction. But the death of Jesus is also the witness of the fact that no matter what, God desires to forgive. The cross of Jesus reveals the immensity of God's love and his desire to forgive every sinner.

The following story has been told on many occasions and in various forms, but it bears repeating and reemphasizing as we consider the subject of forgiveness:

Three men are standing on the coast of California. They are ready for an exciting event: a swimming contest to Hawaii! Hawaii is about 2,500 miles away, and there are spectators on the coast there, eagerly waiting to see who will win. The contestants are: Ollie the Olympian, Norm the Normal, and Dag the Doggie-Paddler. And they are off!

Ollie makes a quick dive into the surf and shows his athletic prowess as he braves the cold Pacific waters. Norm jumps over the first few waves and begins to make progress. Dag wades in and immediately gets knocked over at the first crest of a wave. He comes up, gasping, and attempts again. Down he goes, under the water, finally reappearing with cries for help. Fortunately, a lifeguard can easily reach him and Dag is pulled to the sand in safety. In the meantime, Ollie is still making great strides as he does beautiful breaststrokes out into the deep waters of the ocean. Norm, on the other hand, has been swimming for some time and is growing tired. His practice of swimming a few laps every day has gotten him this far, but he can go no further. He swims a decent distance from land but has lost his steam. At last, the lifeguard climbs into his raft and brings Norm in to dry land. And now Ollie is the only contestant left. He is swimming as if his life depends on it! In fact, Ollie goes so far that he can't be seen from those lined up on the shore. He swims many miles, but in the end, even Ollie begins to grow weary. His heroic effort is applauded when he is returned safely in the lifeguard's boat.

From the perspective of all the observers on the California coast, Ollie is the winner and Dag is the loser. Ollie wins prizes, Norm sheepishly accepts second place and poor Dag hangs his head in shame.

But wait, what about all those people in Hawaii, waiting patiently on the shore? They are craning their necks, waiting to see the arrival of a swimmer. And who do they see? No one. From their perspective, there is no winner. The contest is over and the band goes home.

Let's pretend that your swimming abilities could be compared to your righteousness, your "goodness" before God. If you are like Ollie, you are an Olympian in the moral arena. You honor your parents, never tell lies, and obey the law. You know you aren't perfect, but you're the best of anyone you know. Or perhaps you're more like Norm because you're an OK fellow who makes a few mistakes, but you're no worse than the next guy. Of course, if you are the next guy then you are like Dag. You're down on your luck, you've made all the wrong calls in life and you've lost your morals and have hurt a lot of people and yourself as well.

If you are like Ollie, Norm or Dag, you still need to be "saved" from the treacherous waters of sin. You need a lifeguard. Of course, that lifeguard is Jesus himself, who comes and rescues you no matter where you are and brings you to safety. In fact, if we take the analogy even further, he rescues you and takes you all the way to Hawaii, where you are applauded and paraded, not for being a great swimmer, but for being willing to be saved!

So if swimming to Hawaii represents achieving perfection on our own power and goodness, everyone falls incredibly short of it. From God's perspective, there is really no difference between the three swimmers. This is what they (and all of us!) have to learn—that no matter how good we are in comparison to others, we are all far from perfection. Therefore, we all need a huge amount of forgiveness. And be sure to remember that God is good at forgiving! When you understand how good he is at forgiving you and how much you needed to be forgiven of, you have made it to understanding this love secret. But let's go to another time when Jesus told a parable about how important forgiveness is to loving others. Peter was feeling pretty good about himself when he asked how many times he should forgive. He was in for a surprise (Matthew 18:21-35):

> Then Peter came to Jesus and asked, "Lord, how many times shall I forgive my brother or sister who sins against me? Up to seven times?"
>
> Jesus answered, "I tell you, not seven times, but seventy-seven times.
>
> "Therefore, the kingdom of heaven is like a king who wanted to settle accounts with his servants. As he began the settlement, a man who owed him ten thousand bags of gold was brought to him. Since he was not able to pay, the master ordered that he and his wife and his children and all that he had be sold to repay the debt.
>
> "At this the servant fell on his knees before him. 'Be patient with me,' he begged, 'and I will pay back everything.'

The servant's master took pity on him, canceled the debt and let him go.

"But when that servant went out, he found one of his fellow servants who owed him a hundred silver coins. He grabbed him and began to choke him. 'Pay back what you owe me!' he demanded.

"His fellow servant fell to his knees and begged him, 'Be patient with me, and I will pay it back.'

"But he refused. Instead, he went off and had the man thrown into prison until he could pay the debt. When the other servants saw what had happened, they were outraged and went and told their master everything that had happened.

"Then the master called the servant in. 'You wicked servant,' he said, 'I canceled all that debt of yours because you begged me to. Shouldn't you have had mercy on your fellow servant just as I had on you?' In anger his master handed him over to the jailers to be tortured, until he should pay back all he owed.

"This is how my heavenly Father will treat each of you unless you forgive your brother or sister from your heart."

Wow, those concluding remarks are strong words from our loving and kind Jesus. The ending of his lesson is ironic, considering the servant could never have paid back what he owed from inside a prison. Jesus is making a strong statement that includes a command, not just a good idea. He used a parable that is extreme to reveal to us an extreme lesson. Compare yourself to the first servant. You have no clout and no collateral. You're in debt up to your ears. You beg for mercy, and somehow you graciously receive it. After you receive this good news, you run into someone who owes you one or two bucks. Instantly you violently attack him, demanding your money. What on earth?

Why would you act so maliciously? There are two possible reasons:

1. You don't really believe your debt has been cancelled. You are filled with dread that one day the lender will come

knocking on your door, demanding payment. You live with that dread and take it out on the one who owes you a little. You have to take what you can get!

2. Change the story a little, and assume that a bit of time has passed between the time your debt was cancelled and your encounter with the other servant. You have forgotten, or the memory is dim, about your own debt problems. Because the debt forgiveness was so long ago, your appreciation has faded, and the few dollars owed to you are exaggerated in your mind as an immense financial amount.

Now let's consider what we need to learn from this parable about forgiveness. In your own life, why would you be unwilling to forgive another human being?

1. You don't understand how much God has forgiven you. In the back of your mind, you always consider that God is holding your sins over your head. You believe that eventually God will "come to his senses" and announce your guilt. Living with that fear and dread brings out the worst in you; you take it out on others.

2. The sins you feel the most guilty about were a long time ago. You asked for forgiveness and believed in God's grace. You've changed your life and the memory of those sins has faded. You aren't that person any more, and you're glad of that, but the intensity of gratefulness has declined through the years. Now you see other people's faults and sins and you have forgotten how much God has forgiven you.

KAY: *The first time I saw the scar on Randy's chest was at a picnic. Several of the college students were together at a lake, and Randy, shirtless, was rowing a boat. The scar was a vivid red line from the top of his chest down to his abdomen. It was a shocking reminder of the surgery he had undergone for cancer just a couple of years earlier. As time has gone on, the scar remains, but it's not as noticeable. It has faded with time. But it's* *still there. Once, after several years of marriage, Randy and I were at a beach when a gentleman came up to Randy and introduced himself as a cardiac surgeon. He politely asked about the scar on Randy's chest. I was a little surprised; I'd become so accustomed to it that I hardly even thought about it. Even today, I'm sometimes startled to remember what that scar represents. As Randy talked about in Love Secret 1, the scar remains as a reminder of the disease that could have taken his life. But at the same time, the scar reminds me that his life was saved! Even though so much time and healing has occurred, I never want to forget how close Randy came to death. It makes him, and me, appreciate life so much more.*

I was baptized into Christ over forty-one years ago. On that day, my sins—past, present and future—were forgiven. I never want to forget the mercy that was given to me and continues to be given to me. Just like Randy's scar, the memory of that day makes me appreciate the life God has given me. By remaining aware of the great amount of forgiveness I've received, I can grow more and more in my forgiveness toward others.

If you are wrestling with the concept of forgiveness, you are not alone. When Jesus demands forgiveness, he is not proclaiming it a simple and easy thing. But it's crucial. It's at the crux of the Christian faith. You might not understand how to do it; perhaps something's happened to you that is so hurtful you need help to get to the place of forgiveness. But you can't refuse to go there. If you say in your heart, "I will never forgive..." then you are not following Christ. That may sound harsh, but there's no other way to put it. Refusal to forgive is disobedience to Jesus.

This book is written for those who want to follow Jesus. It's written for people who want to know the radical love of God and want to give that radical love to others. Radical love is found in forgiveness, and forgiveness is radical. Don't let your perspective be framed by the thinking of those who aren't following Jesus. "She hurt me; I'll hurt her back." "I'll get even." "He'll be sorry." "I will never speak to him again." These are statements made by people who don't know Christ, or if they do, they don't know what he stood for and what he taught. We are so easily influenced! But we must remember that if we want to love the way Jesus did, we have to forgive the way Jesus did.

When we consider having a radical love, it begins with radical forgiveness. Most of us are finally ready to forgive if we think the person who hurt us understands our pain. But that's not Jesus' way of forgiveness. When Jesus suffered on the cross, he exhibited forgiveness even for those who caused his torment. He was stripped and humiliated, and while those who carried out the crucifixion were gambling for his clothes he prayed, *"Father, forgive them, for they do not know what they are doing"* (Luke 23:34). This was the time of Jesus' greatest suffering, yet his words display compassion. "But Jesus," we might say, "they *did* know what they were doing! They drove the nails into your hands and feet! They spit at you and mocked you! How can you say they didn't know?" Jesus' answer to that would probably be that the soldiers did not know the gravity of their actions. And before we accuse again, can we not look at ourselves? Do we fully understand our own sins and what we did to Jesus? Yet Jesus freely forgives.

As those who have dedicated their lives to the cause of Christ, we must embrace forgiveness like never before. We are God's *"chosen people, holy and dearly loved,"* says the apostle Paul. He urges us: *"clothe yourselves with compassion, kindness, humility, gentleness and patience. Bear with each other and forgive one another....**Forgive as the Lord forgave you***" (Colossians 3:12–13, emphasis added). In the same way, Paul wrote to the church in Ephesus: *"Get rid of all bitterness, rage and anger, brawling and slander, along with every form of malice. Be kind and compassionate to one another, **forgiving each other, just as in Christ God forgave you**"* (Ephesians 4:31–32, emphasis added).

How does Jesus forgive you? He forgives you freely. He forgives you completely. He forgives your sins. He forgives your weaknesses. He forgives your personality quirks. He forgives the sins of the past. He forgives the sins of the present. He forgives the sins of the future. He forgives the little remarks and the imperceptible eye-rolling and the frustrated sighs and the mutterings under your breath. He forgives when you forget to do the right thing. He forgives when you say the wrong thing. He forgives the big things and the small things. That's how Jesus forgives you.

Can you do the same for others? The command is to *"forgive as the Lord forgave you."* The problem is that we only forgive as we perceive the Lord has forgiven us. Let's be reminded of our love secret:

Forgiven Little = Loves Little = Forgives Little
Forgiven Much = Loves Much = Forgives Much

How much do you see yourself needing to be forgiven? How much do you really think you have been forgiven? Just how good do you think you are?

RANDY: I need forgiveness from God and a whole lot of it! In fact, I am in desperate need of God's forgiveness. Yet I have never been drunk, I have never used drugs, I never had premarital sex, I have never committed adultery and I have never murdered anyone. And, on top of that, I became a Christian pretty early in life—at seventeen. The "big" and "obvious" and "loud" sins have never been a huge part of my life. But I am a great quiet sinner—before and after becoming a Christian. I have lied, I have lusted after women and possessions, I have been jealous, I have put myself first before God, I have been mean, I have been angry, I have looked down on others, I have been greedy, I have thought myself better than others, I've been selfish, I've been uncaring...and the list could go on and on! Both as an unredeemed sinner and as a redeemed sinner, I am in desperate need of forgiveness, in desperate need of a Savior. So, it's not the person who has had the "big," "loud" sins forgiven who will automatically love much. In fact, I've seen plenty of people with those kinds of sins who love very little. Anyone who perceives how huge a sinner they are before a holy and righteous God will love much because they have been forgiven much. I love God so much that I strive to love others. And when I am hurt and need to forgive, I go to work on that. Sometimes it's an easy thing to do. Sometimes I find it a very difficult task because of the depth of the pain and disappointment. But I do my best to get to the land of forgiveness and to stay there!

Can you make it your aim to give grace and mercy the way Jesus gives it to you? Can you overlook the little hurts and the big ones? Can you decide not to get your feelings hurt so much? Can you decline to talk about what someone else did to you? In fact, can you do good to someone who has hurt you?

KAY: When you are falling in love, everything that your beloved does is important. You watch for all the signs to make sure he feels the same way you do. Every look and word is examined and reexamined with a thrill of excitement and fear. So, it was with breathless anticipation that I waited for my short interaction with Randy after church one night when we had just started dating. I was in my car in the parking lot, with a friend of mine in the passenger seat. Randy came out to the car, and I eagerly awaited his words of romance. I was ready to gush. But lo and behold, Randy was distracted. Something was on his mind (you mean, something other than me occupied his thoughts?) and he was a little abrupt. We exchanged just a few words and then he turned to go. I watched his back as he walked away, surprised and embarrassed.

"He just hurt your feelings, didn't he?" I was startled by the voice from the friend in the car with me. I had almost forgotten that she was there. "Yes," I admitted. "He certainly did!"

My friend spoke with calm authority. "Now you have to do something nice for him." She went on to teach me a valuable lesson. "Whenever someone hurts you, it's an opportunity for you to become like Christ."

Although that advice went contrary to my human nature, it was true and valid. How could I claim to be like Jesus if I wasn't able to forgive such a little injury? Her wise words have stayed with me through the years; they are a beacon of light that guide me when forgiveness is hard.

If you want to love like Jesus, you can start with learning how to forgive. Sometimes even the little petty things are hard to get over, but if you can't do that, how will you learn to forgive the bigger hurts in life? Remember, forgiveness is given to others in proportion to the amount we personally perceive forgiveness is needed and has been given to us. This is a training and learning process. You have to practice forgiveness. It won't come naturally all the time. But the more you practice, the more you make progress. So the more you recognize you've been forgiven, the more progress in love and forgiveness you can make. As 1 Peter 4:8 proclaims: *"Above all, love each other deeply, because love covers over a multitude of sins."* Love Secret 2 is crucial if we want to have radical love! Remember...

Forgiven Little = Loves Little = Forgives Little
Forgiven Much = Loves Much = Forgives Much

LOVE SECRET 3

Self-Denial Love

In 1965 a song with lyrics by Hal David, music by Burt Bacharach and sung by Jackie DeShannon hit the airwaves that spoke to the hearts of millions as it quickly rose on the top 100 chart. It was entitled, "What the World Needs Now Is Love."

And now over fifty years later, the message still rings true. We do need love. But, what kind of love do we need? There are four Greek words for love, and three of them are used in the Bible.

1. *Eros* **Love:** This is sexual or passionate love. It is the state that we call "being in love." It is the kind of love which lovers are "in." We get the English word erotic from this. This word is not found in the Bible.

2. *Storge* **Love:** This is affectionate love. It gives thanks for and takes delight in the objects of its admiration. It is the love and affection that naturally occurs between parents and children. It exists between husbands and wives in a good marriage and it can exist between siblings. It occurs only once in the Bible and only as a compound word. It is found in Romans 12:10 in the word *philostorgos*, which is a compound word made up of *philos* (the noun form of *phileo*) and *storge*. It is a very important verse that directs us to be very loving and kind to each other.

3. *Phileo* **Love:** This is friendship love. It is that deep sense of togetherness and joy two people have with one another. It implies a strong emotional connection. In John 21, as Jesus was confronting Peter, he asked him two times if he had *agape* love for him. Both times Peter answered saying

he had *phileo* love for Jesus. Jesus was asking Peter if he loved him with the love of God—a love that may require sacrifice. Or put another way, Peter was being asked if he was willing to do things for Jesus that he would not want to do and would not feel like doing. Peter answered by saying he wanted to remain a close associate, a companion and a true friend. The third time Jesus asked Peter if he had *phileo* love for him. And Peter answered saying he did have *phileo* love for him—that he wanted to be emotionally connected as great friends. We believe a main point Jesus was making is that both aspects of love would be required. They would need to be good friends and Peter would have to do his will even when it meant hardship and sacrifice to the point of death.

4. ***Agape* Love:** This love expresses itself in a devotion that longs to give what is best and to serve regardless of the cost. This is the word that refers to the love of God and is to be one of the kinds of love we are to have for people. *Agape* is the very nature of God, for God is love (1 John 4:7–12, 16b). The way to understand *agape* is that it can be known from the action it initiates. Today, people think of love as a feeling, but that is not necessarily the case with agape love. *Agape* is love because of what it does, not because of how it feels. For God so loved (*agape*) that he gave his Son. It did not feel good to God to do that, but it was the loving thing to do. Jesus so loved (*agape*) that he gave his life. He did not want to die, but because he loved, he did what God required. So *agape* love is not simply an impulse generated from feelings. Instead, *agape* love is an exercise of the will, a deliberate choice. This is why God can command us to love our enemies. He is not commanding us to have a good feeling for our enemies, but to act in a loving way toward them. Once again, *agape* love is related to obedience and commitment, and not necessarily to feeling and emotion. This does not imply that *agape* love cannot have feelings attached to it. In

fact, the best situation occurs when the loving thing to do is also what we want to do.

So what the world needs now is still, as the song says, LOVE SWEET LOVE—it is the only thing that there's JUST TOO LITTLE OF. If a person is going to have a fulfilling Christian life, be obedient to God and have an incredible fellowship with other Christians, they must embrace and have in their lives the last three kinds of love. We need *agape* love because some of the things that God requires of us are not fun or easy; it will require personal sacrifice to be obedient. We need *phileo* love because we need true friends to stand with us, people who are emotionally connected to us and with whom we can share our deepest thoughts and feelings. And we need *storge* love because we need this deep family affection that comforts us and helps us feel connected to all our spiritual family.

A major key to open the door for love is self-denial. Self-denial demonstrates itself by servanthood. If you want to live, you have to die. It's a paradox. If you want to live a life of love daily, you have to die to yourself daily. This does not contradict the truth that we must love ourselves. Self-love is necessary so that we are able to love others. This will be defined and discussed in the next love secret. But our focus for the moment is on the fact that love and selfishness are polar opposites. To the degree that we are full of selfishness, to that degree we are not full of love. As our selfishness decreases, our love increases. Or it could be stated, as our self-denial increases, so increases our capacity to love. Then, as we have a greater love, we become a greater servant. In other words, the demonstration of a person increasing in love is a person increasing in serving. And so our Love Secret 3 would look like this:

As You Increase in Self-Denial, You Increase in Love
As You Increase in Love, You Increase in Serving

Let's look at John 12:23–26 and Luke 9:23–24 and see the similarity of words.

Jesus replied, "The hour has come for the Son of Man

to be glorified. Very truly I tell you, unless a kernel of wheat falls to the ground and dies, it remains only a single seed. But if it dies, it produces many seeds. Anyone who loves their life will lose it, while anyone who hates their life in this world will keep it for eternal life. Whoever serves me must follow me; and where I am, my servant also will be. My Father will honor the one who serves me." (John 12:23–26)

Then he said to them all: "Whoever wants to be my disciple must deny themselves and take up their cross daily and follow me. For whoever wants to save their life will lose it, but whoever loses their life for me will save it." (Luke 9:23–24)

If you take any kind of seed and bury it in the ground allowing it to die, what it produces is something much more glorious than the original single seed. Yes! At the death of every seed, something much greater is born and brought into existence, like a beautiful, giant oak tree from a small, single acorn. So it was with Jesus and so it will be with us. When we let our one seed (life) die, it will give life to many (many seeds). How does a seed die? The hard shell must be broken through. And how does this happen? A person must let the love of God cut deeply enough in their heart to burst open the shell, the surrounding hardness. The hardness exists because of our selfishness. It lives in our lives in a variety of ways. We will look at some of the ways it is manifested. But remember, self-denial is a positive command because it leads to living the selfless life we were created to live. It leads to living the best life possible. It means being transformed and changed. It means living in a state of fulfilment and satisfaction.

RANDY: *I am a person who has to always watch my diet or I would rapidly gain weight. That is my body's tendency. And yet I love to eat! I like chocolate peanut M&Ms; I like angel food cake with chocolate icing; I like mint chip ice cream; I like rolls and pastries; I like lobster with melted butter (and I believe in total immersion, not sprinkling with that butter!). I like junk food, whether it be McDonalds' french fries or Krispy Kreme Donuts or Oreo cookies or Lay's potato chips. The list could go on. I have to deny myself. I have to say no to things I would like and enjoy. It's not* *always easy and at times it's just downright tough. I would even be happy (in the moment) to eat all the food I wanted and toss to the wind any self-denial. But in the long haul, I know that I am more satisfied, happier and feel better about myself by the result of saying "no" or "not now" or "in moderation." I have found that self-denial is a key to achieving many things in this life both physically and spiritually. And, by the way, dieting only works if it's daily. The same is true with self-denial!*

Self-denial (dealing with our selfishness) always produces something better and greater. Anything great in life requires self-denial. Becoming a great musician takes self-denial. Becoming a great athlete takes self-denial. Becoming a great student takes self-denial. Having a great marriage takes self-denial. Having a great family takes self-denial. It all takes saying no to the lesser things that could bring some momentary joy and pleasure and saying yes to what is usually harder, more challenging, more demanding and takes more discipline. And the greatest thing in life—LOVE—also takes self-denial. We were created to be like Jesus and to live a life of love. It only happens through daily self-denial.

Salvation is obtained in one act. We are baptized into Christ for the forgiveness of our sins with faith, repentance and with the decision to make Jesus our Lord (Acts 2:38; Romans 10:9). Spirituality, on the other hand, is attained through a lifetime of consistent effort to transform our total person from who we have been into who Jesus is. Since spirituality is becoming like Jesus, and Jesus is love, then in this life we are to become more and more loving. This change and transformation must be from the inside out. You can't just paste on love.

DENY TO FLY

So let's go deep. Let's first look at six aspects of self (selfishness) that must be continually put to death so that love can continually spread its wings and fly!

1. **Self-Gratification**—This is living by pleasure instead of by principle. It's doing what feels good at the moment. It produces an undisciplined, unorganized, unproductive and unfaithful life. It leads to an impure life with undealt-with lust and sexual immorality.

But when there is denial of self-gratification a person will not live in a guilt-ridden or overwhelmed state. They will feel great about themselves because they are living right. They will be righteous and ready to be used by God and equipped to love others.

2. **Self-Justification**—This finds a person rationalizing their sin and problems. They are not willing to take 100% responsibility for who they are. The tendency is to shift blame. They blame their background, their family, those who have sinned against them, their circumstances or even people who have tried to help them. This leads to a lonely life. They will not accept the truth that they are who they are because they have chosen it.

But when there is denial of self-justification a person can start to change because they start to take personal responsibility. God can only help change the lives of people who know they are ultimately responsible for their thoughts, feelings and actions. They will become open to getting the help they need to change. All of this opens the door to healthy relationships and love.

3. **Self-Pride**—This person is cocky, arrogant, aloof and independent. They think that advice is given to run and ruin their lives. They are untrusting of God and of people. They are not teachable because ultimately the only one they really trust is themselves. They are easily irritated by correction. They get defensive when someone is contradicting them. They are embarrassed to appear weak. It is difficult to admit they need others. They may even try to make something up to sound intelligent instead of just saying, "I don't know." They find it hard to say, "I was wrong" or "I'm sorry" or "Please forgive me." They find it difficult to confess their sin. They feel superior to others and at the same time threatened by others. They are quick to respond when corrected, questioned or admonished because they feel they are always right. They are not able to hear truth from God's word from just anyone. They tend not to be open about their marriage or family.

But when there is denial of self-pride a person can become teachable and willing to accept help to change to be more like Jesus. They can now develop and sustain lasting, deep and loving relationships in their family and in a circle of friends.

4. **Self-Consciousness**—This is the person who thinks everyone is looking at them and thinking about them. They dwell on themselves. They can even get to the point of being somewhat paranoid thinking people don't like them or people are out to get them. Inside they tend to be scared of people. They are insecure, sometimes in extreme ways.

   But when there is denial of self-consciousness there can be loving relationships as they let others come close. They can be open, honest and vulnerable. They can receive the needed input and encouragement as they step out of their comfort zone and consider others before themselves.

5. **Self-Pity**—Here is the person who feels sorry for themselves and is constantly trying to get others to feel sorry for them, too. They throw pity parties where only three are invited—me, myself and I! They tend toward depression and unhappiness. They draw away from people. They allow past hurts to embitter their present life. They tend to be unforgiving. The way they have handled their hurts is to be unwilling to again give away their heart as they are now protecting themselves and keeping people at a distance. As John Gardner portrays it: "Self-pity is easily the most destructive of the nonpharmaceutical narcotics; it is addictive, gives momentary pleasure and separates the victim from reality."

   But where there is denial of self-pity you will find a happy and outward-focused person. They are appreciative, positive and thankful. They are full of mercy and forgiveness. They are a joy to be around. Their love is magnetic and draws people to Jesus.

6. **Self-Will**—This is the kind of person who rebels against authority. They don't like advice, direction or discipline. They tend to want to do everything their way. When the going gets tough they give in and give up. They do what is easy instead of what is right. This person craves comfort and tends toward greed and materialism.

   But where there is denial of self-will there is a truly humble person. They will know they need God and that they are nothing without him and that God always has the best way. God will be able to use this kind of person to glorify him in extraordinary ways. This person's life will impact and will make a difference. They will have a sacrificial love based on obedience and not on emotion.

The selfless life is the better life by far—it allows us to love and be loved. Selfishness destroys love, and there is a heavy price to pay for a self-centered life. C.S. Lewis puts it this way in his book, *The Four Loves:*

> There is no safe investment. To love at all is to be vulnerable. Love anything, and your heart will certainly be wrung and possibly be broken. If you want to make sure of keeping it intact, you must give your heart to no one, not even to an animal. Wrap it carefully round with hobbies and little luxuries; avoid all entanglements; lock it up safe in the casket or coffin of your selfishness. But in the casket—safe, dark, motionless, airless—it will change. It will not be broken; it will become unbreakable, impenetrable, irredeemable. The alternative to tragedy, or at least to the risk of tragedy, is damnation. The only place outside Heaven where you can be perfectly safe from all the dangers and perturbations of love is Hell.

Yes, selfishness is a living hell. It is not worth the price we must pay for it. It is very costly to be selfless and, yet, it is even more costly to be selfish. Let's be reminded of the scripture in 2 Corinthians 5:14–15 about the selfless life we are motivated to live because of Christ's selfless love for us: *"For Christ's love compels us, because we are convinced that one died for all, and therefore all died. And he died for all, that those who live should* **no longer live for themselves** *but for him who died for them and was raised again"* (emphasis added).

So as we decrease in selfishness or increase in self-denial, we increase in our capacity to love. And as we grow in love we will grow in our capacity to serve. Jesus expects us to take the low position of servants. In fact, love demands it! This is not an extra obligation—it is the obligation of love. It is the very heart of the new relationship with respect to God and to men. Being a servant is the way to express love. When Jesus was alone with his disciples and was soon to be crucified, the Bible says in John 13:1b: *"Having loved his own who were in the world, he loved them to the end."* "End" is the Greek word *telos*, which could be translated "he loved them to the max." How did he demonstrate this love as he was coming to the end of his physical life on earth? He served them by washing their feet. He set the example for them (and for all people for all time) to love each other by serving each other.

> When he had finished washing their feet, he put on his clothes and returned to his place. "Do you understand what I have done for you?" he asked them. "You call me 'Teacher' and 'Lord,' and rightly so, for that is what I am. Now that I, your Lord and Teacher, have washed your feet, you also should wash one another's feet. I have set you an example that you should do as I have done for you. Very truly I tell you, no servant is greater than his master, nor is a messenger greater than the one who sent him. Now that you know these things, you will be blessed if you do them." (John 13:12–17)

CALL TO ALL

The person who deeply loves Jesus will be willing to humble himself and become a servant, loving the people around him. This is God's call to all. To best understand the servant position, there are four important preliminary points:

1. **Two Kinds of Servants**—In the Old Testament Scriptures, we find two kinds of servants. The hired servant had wages paid to them and they maintained certain rights. The other type of servant was a bondservant or slave. The bondservant had no rights. No slave in the Roman Empire could be a citizen or have the rights that came with that status. A slave could not own anything. A slave could not give testimony or be defended in a court of law. A slave had no time that they could call their own. They received no wages and they had no right to appeal anything they were told to do. In the New Testament, the Greek word (*doulos*) for "servant" of the Lord is not the hired servant, it is the bondservant. It is the slave. The slave is the absolute property of the master and is to be treated and disposed of just as the master wishes.

2. ***Doulos* Means Slave**—The Greek word *doulos* means slave. There is no getting past it. It does not mean servant, worker, hired hand or helper. Yet the "slave" word was basically removed from our English translations except for the places where it refers to the position of an actual physical slave or to an inanimate object, as in "slaves to righteousness" or "slaves to sin." In the New Testament, the Greek word for slave is used about 150 times in all its forms, yet it is translated as slave only a few of those times. (Some of the non-English translations do better using the word "slave.") Why was this done? Because there were those who thought that the word "slave" had too many negative connotations for a follower of Christ. Instead, the word "servant" or "bondservant" was used. This was done in the time of the first English translations in the sixteenth century with John Calvin and John Knox and other translators who were putting together the Geneva Bible. They considered that using the word "slave" would be too derogatory, too degrading and too demeaning. Yet the Bible teaches over and over again that any follower of Jesus is a *doulos* or slave.

It is interesting to note that in the first century, slavery was a massive institution. There were twelve million slaves in the Mediterranean world, and one out of every five people in the Roman Empire was a slave. Yet the Holy Spirit was not fearful or reluctant about using the word "slave" to describe a follower of Jesus. Obviously it was an important concept with which to understand just who a follower of Christ is.

3. **Jesus Was a Slave**—A Christian is one who chooses to be a slave of the one willing to be a slave.

In your relationships with one another, have the same mindset as Christ Jesus:
    Who, being in very nature God,
        did not consider equality with God something to be
        used to his own advantage;
        rather, he made himself nothing
    by taking the very nature of a servant [doulos or slave!],
        being made in human likeness. (Philippians 2:5–7)

Jesus gave up his rights. He was willing to be treated as the will of the Father and the evil intent of men might decree. He demonstrated what it meant to be a servant (*doulos*) or bondservant or—the correct word—slave. In the passage concerning the washing of the apostle's feet, it was the master serving his slaves.

4. **Slave to Others**—Our servanthood (being a slave) to Jesus is to express itself in our servanthood (being a slave) to others. *"For what we preach is not ourselves, but Jesus Christ as Lord [master], and ourselves as your servants [slaves] for Jesus' sake"* (2 Corinthians 4:5).

An unwillingness to serve others in costly, humbling ways is an unwillingness to serve Jesus. This may sound harsh and too absolute, but it's true. Following Jesus is so much more than man's feeble attempt to feel better about himself. So much of Christianity in today's world is about feeling good without much regard to obedience to Christ. Since being a slave of Christ with *agape* love does not always feel good, this vital truth about Christianity is often obscured or deleted. This will be further explored in "Love Secret 5: Obedient Love."

NEVER TO SEVER

Now let's apply the servant/slave concept more personally to our lives. Jesus told a story that clearly describes a *doulos,* a slave:

> "Suppose one of you has a servant [doulos] plowing or looking after the sheep. Will he say to the servant [doulos] when he comes in from the field, 'Come along now and sit down to eat'? Won't he rather say, 'Prepare my supper, get yourself ready and wait on me while I eat and drink; after that you may eat and drink'? Will he thank the servant [doulos] because he did what he was told to do? So you also, when you have done everything you were told to do, should say, 'We are unworthy servants [doulos]; we have only done our duty.'" (Luke 17:7–10)

This passage, in context, is not primarily trying to teach what a servant is or is not. The primary purpose of this story is to answer a question asked by the apostles on how to increase their faith. (See "Faith Secret 10: Increasing Faith" in the book *Radical Faith—10 Faith Secrets.*) But certainly this passage does give great insight to us concerning the important lesson of what a servant or slave of Christ is. We must never sever ourselves from these seven signs of being a slave:

SEVEN SIGNS OF A SERVANT/SLAVE

Sign #1—Servants/slaves must be willing to have one thing on top of another put upon them without any consideration being given to them. On top of a hard day in the field they are to immediately prepare the master's meal. On top of that they are to wait on the table. All of this is to be done before they get their own food and without murmurings or bitterness. The moment they start to complain they are acting as if they have rights, and a servant/slave has no rights.

Sign #2—In all that servants/slaves do, they must be willing to remain unthanked. There can be no self-pity if they are unappreciated. There can be no complaining if they are not recognized. They exist to serve. A servant/slave expects nothing.

Sign #3—Having done all to serve, the servant/slave must not charge the one they have served with selfishness. There is no charge from the servant/slave that the master is being inconsiderate. The servant/slave exists to serve others.

Sign #4—There can be no grounds for pride or self-congratulation but they must only express that they are unworthy servants/slaves. They are to understand that within themselves they are unworthy to serve God or man. They must know that it is only by the power and the grace of God that they have accomplished and done anything good.

Sign #5—The servant/slave admits that they have not done more than was their duty to do. God initially made mankind to be his servant and to be servants of one another. Man's sin has simply consisted in his refusal to be God's servant/slave and therefore a refusal to serve his fellow man in a godly way. The servant is simply restoring himself to the position of servant/slave to God. This is what he was created and redeemed for. *"Do nothing out of selfish ambition or vain conceit. Rather, in humility value others above yourselves, not looking to your own interests but each of you to the interests of the others"* (Philippians 2:3–4).

Sign #6—Servants/slaves anticipate needs and then take initiative. The master assumes that all the needs of the sheep or the field are being taken care of by the servant. So, just having a willingness to serve when asked is not the whole of being a servant. And just asking if there is some-thing to be done to help every now and then is not the whole of being a servant. A servant/slave consistently finds out what needs to be done and then consistently does it.

Sign #7—Servants/slaves are willing to meet all the needs of all others. They are to do *"everything"* they were told or required to do for all in the master's household. They have not come to the point where they feel they are too good to serve certain people. They don't just serve their family or close friends or those who agree with them. They serve all, or they are not a servant of Jesus at all.

The servant is to be concerned for all kinds of needs. These would include physical, spiritual, and emotional needs.

Physical needs would include such things as providing food, clothing or shelter. It may involve cleaning the house, washing clothes, doing the dishes, mowing the lawn, shov-eling snow or raking leaves. It may be helping with home-work or repairing a car or doing the shopping.

Spiritual needs would include teaching the lost and fellow disciples the truths of the Bible. It would include cor-recting and training and encouraging.

Emotional needs would be such things as weeping with those who weep and rejoicing with those who rejoice. It could be going and talking to the lonely, possibly a widow or those who are sick. It may be supplying some emotional needs of the fatherless by taking an interest in their life and well-being. It may be holding a hand, which says clearly that you care. It's sharing dreams together, believing in a person and offering to be a genuine friend to someone.

LOVE TO LOVE

Love is not just something we do. It's not just doing the right thing in the right way at the right time. Love is to be who we are. We are to be God's people who love to love! 1 John 3:16–18 puts it this way:

This is how we know what love is: Jesus Christ laid

down his life for us. And we ought to lay down our lives for our brothers and sisters. If anyone has material posses- sions and sees a brother or sister in need but has no pity on them, how can the love of God be in that person? Dear children, let us not love with words or speech but with ac- tions and in truth.

With this in mind, let's be who we were created to be. Let's not be like this would-be disciple:

THE PADDED CROSS
(the musings of a would-be disciple)
Unknown author/Adapted

"Well, here I am, Lord. You said, 'Take up your cross' and I'm here to do it! It's not easy, you know, this self-denial thing. I mean to go through with it though. YES SIR! I'll bet you wish more people were willing to be disciples like me. I've counted the cost, surrendered my life...it's not an easy road.

"You mind if I look over these crosses? I was wondering if there are any vinyl-padded ones. I'm thinking of attracting others, you understand, and if I could show them a comfort- able cross I'm sure I could win a lot more. Got to keep up with the population explosion and all. And I need something durable so I can treasure it always. Oh, is there one that's sort of flat so it would fit in my pocket? One should not be too obvious.

"Funny, there doesn't seem to be much choice here. Just that coarse, rough wood. I mean, that would hurt! Don't you have something more distinctive, Lord? I can tell you right now none of my friends are going to be impressed by this shoddy workmanship. They'll think I'm a nut or some- thing! And my family will be just mortified.

"What's that? It's either one of these or forget the whole

thing? But Lord, I want to be your disciple! But you don't understand...nobody lives that way today! Who's going to be attracted by this self-denial bit? And who really wants to be a slave? And, on top of all that, it's just too daily. I mean I want to, but let's not overdo it! Start getting radical like this and they'll have me off to the funny farm...know what I mean?

"I mean, being a disciple is challenging and exciting and I want to do it, but I do have some rights, you know! Now let's see. NO BLOOD, OK? I just can't stand the sight or thought of that, LORD...LORD?...LORD?

"Now where do you suppose HE went?!"

God has his standards. God has his truth. God has his way. God has what the world needs now...love sweet love! Disciples need to DENY TO FLY—if we deny ourselves we can fly high with love; we need to hear the CALL TO ALL—hear the call to love by becoming a servant/slave to God and to others; we must have the conviction NEVER TO SEVER—never sever ourselves from the signs of serving love; and we must LOVE TO LOVE—we must love serving as a demonstration and outcome of our love.

And so, Love Secret 3 is...

As You Increase in Self-Denial, You Increase in Love
As You Increase in Love, You Increase in Serving

LOVE SECRET 4

Self Love

If you have been anywhere in the presence of a little girl any time over the last few years you have probably heard a heartfelt rendition of the song "Let It Go!" The song has been translated, adapted, mixed and imitated by professionals and amateurs alike. It's a music phenomenon. "Let It Go" is from a Disney movie called *Frozen*, which tells the tale of two sisters, Elsa and Anna. In spite of the "curse" that Elsa suffers, Anna is devoted to her sister and eventually her love for Elsa saves the day. The story is lovely, but did you know that it is based on another story that has an even deeper meaning?

The Snow Queen, written in 1884 by Hans Christian Anderson, begins with an evil troll who made a magic mirror. This mirror was not one that showed a true reflection, but instead revealed a distorted image of everything it reflected. Instead of reflecting the good and beautiful aspects of people and things, it magnified their bad and ugly aspects. The troll, along with his pupils, took the mirror around the world and delighted in distorting everything. One day they decided to take the mirror to heaven, in order to make fools of the angels and God. But as they were carrying it up into the sky, it slipped from their grasp and fell back to the earth, shattering into millions of splinters, some no larger than a grain of sand. The glass slivers were blown about and fell into the eyes of some of the people on earth. Their eyes became like the troll mirror itself, seeing only bad and ugly things.

The fairy tale reveals the truth that the wrong perspective changes everything. Jesus addressed this problem in his Sermon on the Mount: *"The eye is the lamp of the body. If your eyes are healthy, your whole body will be full of light. But if your eyes are unhealthy, your whole body will be full of darkness. If then the light within you is darkness, how great is that darkness!"* (Matthew 6:22–23).

Our viewpoint can make everything dark and grim and ugly, or it can make things full of light. This is true regarding our vision of the world and of those in it, but it's also true about our vision of ourselves! How does God want us to view ourselves? Did Jesus come to earth to make us feel bad about ourselves? Have our eyes been stricken with "troll mirror pieces" when it comes to our perspective about ourselves?

Without a doubt, we must see ourselves as sinners in need of the grace of God. We know that we are nothing without him and his love. However, too many people who have received God's grace and forgiveness still do not see themselves the way God does. To not accept God's view of ourselves is another way of denying his love. Without accepting that love, it is impossible to love others.

God created man and woman in his image, in his likeness (Genesis 1:26). In fact, human beings are his crowning achievement! Being made in the image of God does not mean that God has a physical resemblance to men or women; otherwise we would all look alike. But it does mean that there is something of God in each one of us. We are created to possess an eternal soul. All of our intellect, personality, ability to reason, to forgive, to create—all of these are from God and make us uniquely human. God had a purpose in creating men and women: we were created to reflect him! What an honor and a glory, to be God's representation on the earth. If you are a parent, don't you love it when someone says, "Your son/daughter looks just like you"? There is such a sense of pride when another human being reflects you and reminds someone of you! That's the goal that God has for you. That is the first step in loving yourself. You are created in the image of God.

God declared that the whole of his creation was "very good" (Genesis 1:31). That included the human race. Not only did he create us in his image, he also says that he *"crowned them with glory and honor"* (Psalm 8:5). We are *"fearfully and wonderfully made"* (Psalm 139:14). In the act of creation, wisdom is portrayed as the craftsman by the side of God,

> *...filled with delight day after day,*
> *rejoicing always in his presence,*
> *rejoicing in his whole world*
> *and delighting in mankind."* (Proverbs 8:30–31)

In other words, it's a *wise* thing to delight in humanity!

Belittling ourselves, self-demeaning talk and self-loathing are the opposite of self-love, and they are the opposite of how God wants you to view yourself. There are many causes for low self-esteem and low self-worth. Some of the causes are things beyond our control, such as traumatic incidents in childhood or being bombarded throughout youth by negative talk. These are not easy things to overcome, but to have the right kind of self-love, we must see ourselves from God's eyes. Even with the invasion of Satan's schemes, we have hope. Not only were we created by God, but we were recreated in Christ Jesus. *"For we are God's handiwork, created in Christ Jesus to do good works, which God prepared in advance for us to do"* (Ephesians 2:10). Can you begin to see yourself as God's masterpiece?

THE TOUCH OF THE MASTER'S HAND

Myra Brooks Welch

'Twas battered and scarred, and the auctioneer
Thought it scarcely worth his while
To waste much time on the old violin,
But held it up with a smile.
"What am I bidden, good folks," he cried,
"Who'll start the bidding for me?"
"A dollar, a dollar," then, two! Only two?
"Two dollars, and who'll make it three?
"Three dollars, once; three dollars, twice;
Going for three..." But no,
From the room, far back, a grey-haired man
Came forward and picked up the bow;
Then wiping the dust from the old violin,
And tightening the loose strings,
He played a melody pure and sweet
As a caroling angel sings.

The music ceased, and the auctioneer,
With a voice that was quiet and low,

Said: "What now am I bid for the old violin?"
And he held it up with the bow.
"A thousand dollars, and who'll make it two?
Two thousand! And who'll make it three?
Three thousand, once; three thousand, twice;
And going and gone," said he.
The people cheered, but some of them cried,
"We do not quite understand,
What changed its worth?" Swift came the reply:
"The touch of a master's hand."

And many a man with life out of tune
And battered and scarred with sin
Is auctioned cheap to the thoughtless crowd,
Much like the old violin.
A mess of potage, a glass of wine;
A game—and he travels on.
He is going once, and going twice,
He's going and almost gone.
But the Master comes and the foolish crowd
Never can quite understand
The worth of a soul and the change that's wrought
By the touch of the Master's hand.

As those who have been "touched by the Master's hand," we
exhibit God's glory and beauty. The degree to which we can see that
glory and beauty within ourselves determines the degree to which we
can see it in others. Hence,

Greater Love for Self *Allows* Greater Love for Others
Lesser Love for Self *Allows* Lesser Love for Others

Part of the problem with loving ourselves is brought about by the
constant habit of comparing ourselves to others. Sure, other people
can call us higher and be great examples. But God created each person

unique, and if unfair comparisons are made, then we are hindered in reaching the goal of being who God created us to be! It's so easy today to look at others and feel a bit inadequate. You might be a decent cook, but then you watch a television show like *Chopped* and ask yourself, "Why can't I cook like that?" Or maybe you've performed some renovations on your house, but then you see an episode of *Fixer Upper* and learn about all the things that you could have done better. Movies and magazines portray only the most beautiful and the most handsome in all their air-brushed, Photoshopped best. But we consider ourselves less beautiful or less handsome because we don't measure up to those outstanding good looks. The fashion and cosmetic industry makes billions of dollars as we purchase products to make us look like someone else!

There is no harm in trying to look your best or be your best. In fact, a symptom of a lack of self-love is found in the person who has let themselves go and gives no concern for hygiene and appearance. We all should do our best to present ourselves in a way that is pleasing to those around us. That shows self-respect as well as respect for those who have to look at us. Even if you are very unhappy with yourself, consider this: Jesus commands us to love our *enemies*! You may call yourself your own worst enemy, yet you are still called to love that enemy!

Jesus calls all his disciples to deny themselves daily. But this does *not* mean that Christians must think poorly of themselves and beat themselves up. Self-denial is ultimately what will bring us the greatest fulfillment in life, because it leads to doing away with sin and to doing what is right. This was explained in Love Secret 3 regarding self-denial. It's a bit of a paradox, but Jesus knew what he was talking about. To follow him, we give up our personal rights, even the right to think ill of ourselves. Ultimately, self-denial brings about right choices and right behavior, not derisive thoughts about ourselves.

Why love yourself? An unhappy, discontent, angry person cannot love another. A person who is discontent with himself and his own life cannot easily give to another. The cravings within him will only lead to relationships where he can grab something from another person. An unfulfilled man or woman will look to be filled by another, instead of looking to fill others' needs.

Jesus was the perfect man with perfect love. But sadly, people in his own time misunderstood the concept of self-love and berated him for being *"a glutton and a drunkard."* They were critical of him for eating and drinking—things that any human being had to do! If Jesus wanted to deny those aspects of humanity he would have lived an austere, closed-off life. But he lived life to the full and shared his life with others. Another accusation made against Jesus was that he was somehow involved in the misuse of funds!

> *While he was in Bethany, reclining at the table in the home of Simon the Leper, a woman came with an alabaster jar of very expensive perfume, made of pure nard. She broke the jar and poured the perfume on his head.*
>
> *Some of those present were saying indignantly to one another, "Why this waste of perfume? It could have been sold for more than a year's wages and the money given to the poor." And they rebuked her harshly.*
>
> *"Leave her alone," said Jesus. "Why are you bothering her? She has done a beautiful thing to me. The poor you will always have with you, and you can help them any time you want. But you will not always have me. She did what she could. She poured perfume on my body beforehand to prepare for my burial. Truly I tell you, wherever the gospel is preached throughout the world, what she has done will also be told, in memory of her."* (Mark 14:3–9)

Some of those around Jesus had a strange conception of how he should be living. But Jesus had no problem with reclining at a feast and allowing a woman to anoint him with expensive oil. He did not say, "No, away with you, woman! I don't deserve this! My body is not important! This is unseemly!" In fact, he said, *"She has done a beautiful thing to me."* The sacredness of his own body, the flesh and blood that had carried him through his mission on earth, was honored. Although Jesus had to give up his life to go to the cross, he did not promote a life of asceticism. In fact, although he was willing to suffer, he did not look forward to it with relish, but rather had to pray to prepare for his sacrifice.

Self-love is not an excuse to live in indulgence, nor is it a platform for a life of pampering. Self-love is recognizing and appreciating the precious gift of life that you have, and making the best of it! (All scriptures below have emphasis added.)

> *"Do not seek revenge or bear a grudge against anyone among your people, but love your neighbor **as yourself.** I am the LORD."* (Leviticus 19:18)

> *"'Honor your father and mother,' and 'love your neighbor **as yourself.**'"* (Matthew 19:19)

> *"And the second is like it: 'Love your neighbor **as yourself.**'"* (Matthew 22:39)

> *"The second is this: 'Love your neighbor **as yourself.**' There is no commandment greater than these."* (Mark 12:31)

> *"To love him with all your heart, with all your understanding and with all your strength, and to love your neighbor **as yourself** is more important than all burnt offerings and sacrifices."* (Mark 12:33)

> *"'Love the Lord your God with all your heart and with all your soul and with all your strength and with all your mind'; and, 'Love your neighbor **as yourself.**'"* (Luke 10:27)

> *The commandments, "You shall not commit adultery," "You shall not murder," "You shall not steal," "You shall not covet," and whatever other command there may be, are summed up in this one command: Love your neighbor **as yourself.*** (Romans 13:9)

> *"For the entire law is fulfilled in keeping this one command: Love your neighbor **as yourself.**"* (Galatians 5:14)

"As yourself"—the meaning of the Greek and Hebrew words in these passages is clear: "In the same manner, as if it had been, as if it were, even as, like, to wit, as unto, in comparison to." We MUST understand self-love in order to love our neighbor! Jesus had an

expectation for everyone to have self-love. Love Secret 4 is: If you love yourself God's way, then you can love others God's way.

> **Love Yourself God's Way → Love Others God's Way**

So, how exactly should we love ourselves? It's often been taught that we don't need instructions on how to love ourselves, as it comes very naturally to us. But perhaps that's not really true. Although we cling to ourselves and our wills and our ways, we do need instruction on how to really love ourselves in the way that God intended.

LOVE YOUR BODY

"In the case of an emergency, those parents traveling with small children should put their own oxygen masks on first before assisting their children in putting on their oxygen masks." We hear these instructions each time we fly, and we always wonder if, in the case of a real emergency, we would have the presence of mind to do what is being taught. The instructions, however, are crucial to saving lives. A parent cannot help someone else, even their own child, if they are not breathing!

This same lesson applies to loving ourselves. First, be convinced that loving yourself, in the correct way, is God's will for your life. In the instructions that the apostle Paul gives to husbands and wives for a successful marriage, he includes these words: *"Husbands ought to love their wives as their own bodies. He who loves his wife loves himself. After all, no one ever hated their own body, **but they feed and care for their body**, just as Christ does the church"* (Ephesians 5:28–29, emphasis added).

Paul is implying that any normal person would feed and care for their body. In fact, he compares this to the way Christ nourishes the church. There is no room for austere behavior in a believer. At another time, Paul scolds people for behavior that had no benefit: *"Such regulations indeed have an appearance of wisdom, with their self-imposed worship, their false humility and their **harsh treatment of the body**, but they lack any value in restraining sensual indulgence"* (Colossians 2:23, emphasis added). In his letter to the church in Corinth, Paul reminds the Christians, *"Do you not know your bodies are temples of the Holy Spirit, who is in you, whom you have received from God? You are* *not your own; you were bought at a price. Therefore **honor God with your bodies***" (1 Corinthians 6:19–20, emphasis added).

Your body is the house in which God has chosen to dwell. He lives within the believer who has committed to make Jesus Lord of their life. Doesn't that make you think a little differently about the body he has given you? If you are a new parent, how much effort and care have you given to the crib or bassinette that will hold your beloved baby? In love, you make sure that it is safe and comfortable. It is a sacred place because of what it holds. The same is true for the body of the Christian!

There is a plethora of books written today about self-care. But it's only when we see the body as God's home that we will be motivated to treat it properly. Indeed, the body is a jar of clay (2 Corinthians 4:7), but it's a jar we have to guard diligently.

There are occasions when the body must suffer to do the will of God. This does not contradict the command to care for ourselves. On the contrary, we make our body our slave in order to obey God. But we can't make it our slave if we have no control over it. If we've let our bodies go to ruin through neglect and dissipation, how will we have the strength to go through challenging times of physical stress when we need to? If we succumb to every single physical whim, we are not doing our bodies any favors. Overeating, oversleeping and lack of exercise are brutal on the body God has given you!

> *Do you not know that in a race all the runners run, but only one gets the prize? Run in such a way as to get the prize. Everyone who competes in the games goes into strict training. They do it to get a crown that will not last, but we do it to get a crown that will last forever. Therefore I do not run like someone running aimlessly; I do not fight like a boxer beating the air. No, I strike a blow to my body and make it my slave so that after I have preached to others, I myself will not be disqualified for the prize.* (1 Corinthians 9:24–27)

Your body is your closest neighbor. Don't ignore it! If it's in need, do what you would do for a neighbor in need. If it's hurting, don't blame it for hurting or get down on it. And if you have been abusing it in any way, stop!

LOVE YOUR JOURNEY

Your journey includes where you have been, where you are and where you are going. If we are to love ourselves in the proper way, we have to make peace even with the places on that path that have been difficult. We have to appreciate where God places us today. And we must look forward to where we are headed, with God, in the future.

> "What a wonderful life I've had! I only wish I'd realized it sooner." —Sidonie Gabrielle Colette

Love Your Past

How do you view your past? Do you look at it through the eyes of regret, bitterness or disappointment? No one can say they haven't had difficulties in life, and some have had it rougher than others. When we can look at our past as the pathway that brought us to God, then no matter where that path began, we can be thankful. Every turn in the road, every obstacle has had a purpose.

We've all learned a lot of lessons in life, and of course there are things we would do differently if we could live our lives over again. Hindsight is 20/20. Can you be a little bit more gentle with the younger you? Can you forgive yourself for your mistakes? God certainly can! If necessary, can you forgive others for the harm they inflicted on you? This is the only path to peace, and to love. Nelson Mandela was imprisoned unjustly for many years in South Africa. He had every reason to be bitter. But he chose a different path. He later wrote these words: "As I walked out the door toward the gate that would lead to my freedom, I knew if I didn't leave my bitterness and hatred behind, I'd still be in prison."

Seeing your path with the right eyes will open the doors to being able to love yourself. When our perspective of the path is blurry with our own regrets and hurts, we are blinded to the ways that God can work.

One of our favorite Christmas movies is *Scrooged*, starring Bill Murray. In this contemporary (1988—is that contemporary enough?) rendition of Charles Dickens' *A Christmas Carol*, the modern-day Scrooge (Frank Cross) is visited by three ghosts on Christmas Eve. The Ghost of Christmas Past is portrayed as an unkempt, cigar-smoking New York cab driver. He takes Frank on a tour of his past and makes him see things that Frank doesn't want to remember. Frank remains hardened to the lessons, and in frustration the cab driver exclaims: "Frank! You don't know who you are, you don't know where you've been, and you don't know where you're going!" Frank was a miserable man under a façade of smooth appearances. His misery exhibited itself in stingy and miserly treatment of others. He had to make peace with himself and with his past. When he caught a true glimpse of his life, he was able to change, becoming a generous (and funny) character.

Make peace with the life you have. Get over the blunders of the past. Be thankful for the good and the bad. Know that your past doesn't define you, but your perspective of it will!

Love Your Present

What about the present? Can you bring yourself to appreciate where you are right now? You might not have everything you'd like to have, but you can learn to be content, whatever the circumstances. Every day is a gift, and we can find something beautiful in everything around us. Moses left us some powerful words that are found in Psalm 90:

> Teach us to number our days,
>   that we may gain a heart of wisdom.
>
> Relent, LORD! How long will it be?
>   Have compassion on your servants.
> Satisfy us in the morning with your unfailing love,
>   that we may sing for joy and be glad all our days.

Similarly, the prophet Jeremiah framed these words found in chapter 3 of Lamentations:

> Yet this I call to mind
>   and therefore I have hope:
> Because of the LORD's great love we are not consumed,
>   for his compassions never fail.
> They are new every morning;
>   great is your faithfulness.

Both of these prophets recognized, even in the midst of troubles, that each day held great opportunities.

The prayer that we often call The Lord's Prayer contains within it a template of how we can approach each day:

"Our Father in heaven,
Hallowed be Your name,
Your kingdom come,
Your will be done,
On earth as it is in heaven.
Give us today our daily bread.
And forgive us our debts,
As we also have forgiven our debtors.
And lead us not into temptation,
But deliver us from the evil one.
For Yours is the kingdom and the power and the glory
forever. Amen." (Matthew 6:9–13 NKJV)

The prayer begins with the reminder of who God is and continues with the affirmation that the will of God would be preeminent in our lives. This is followed by a request for daily bread, forgiveness and resistance of evil. The prayer concludes with a reminder that God is sovereign over all things. This prayer is a perfect example that can guide us in our daily lives; it has all we need. Memorizing this prayer and repeating it each day (and meaning it) might make all the difference in your life. Try it!

KAY: *I have made it a point to pray The Lord's Prayer every day. Saying the words centers me and reminds me of my place and purpose on earth. I've lately been adding other memorized "prayers" to my daily time with God: Psalm 23 (the Lord is my shepherd) and Psalm 100 (shout for joy to the Lord). At mealtimes, I usually recite some version of Psalm 104 (our eyes look to you and you give us our food at the proper time.... You open your hand and satisfy the desires of every living thing). Praying the Scriptures gives me reminders on a daily basis of all the ways God is working in my life, and it also reminds me of what I want to do with my life.*

You can't love yourself if you don't love today! It's up to you to find ways to love the life God has given you and to love the place you are on in your path. If you are in school today, put yourself into learning. Don't dread it and wish you were finished! If you have small children today, don't wish they were older. They will be soon enough! If you are older and long for the days gone by, remember the words of Solomon: *"Do not say, 'Why were the old days better than these?' For it is not wise to ask such questions"* (Ecclesiastes 7:10).

Love Your Future

The model woman that is praised in Proverbs 31 exudes confidence and strength. She obviously lives in the moment, but how does she view the future? *"She can laugh at the days to come"* (verse 25). She is not worried, fretful or anxious about the future. She does not live with a sense of dread. She lives fully in the day, knowing that God is in control of the future. She can face it with anticipation.

As Christians, we can love our future for several reasons. Because of the promise of Jesus, we know we will never be alone. *"I am with you always,"* he said to his disciples. Beyond the hopes we have for this life, we have great expectation for being with the Lord forever. We are not walking into the sunset, but into the sunrise! The older we get, the closer we are to being with God forever.

What's not to love about your future? Is there anything that God can't handle? Is there any challenge you can't face if he is with you? Any pain that he won't help you bear? A scripture in Hebrews teaches us something about how we can approach the future: *"Let us then approach God's throne of grace with confidence, so that we may receive mercy and find grace to help us in our time of need"* (Hebrews 4:16). Sometimes our worries about the future include some valid concerns. We wonder how we will ever deal with them. But this passage tells us that we will receive what we need *when we need it!* We might not have the strength today to handle something, but God will provide the strength when the time comes. When we say something like, "I won't be able to bear it," we are only going on the measure of strength and grace we have right now, and we forget that God will give us more at just the right time.

You can also look forward to the future because you will always have something to do. As long as you are breathing, God wants to use you! You will never be "past your prime." Think of some of the "old folks" of the Bible: Abraham, Moses, Joshua, Anna, Elizabeth, Sarah—all these and so many more were commissioned for something special when they were way past retirement age! For a disciple of Jesus, the future is bright with possibilities.

RANDY: I'm not getting any younger. In fact, I'm getting older. As I write this I'm turning sixty, but I like to say I'm only fifteen since my birthday comes only once every four years. Yep, I was born on February 29. The funny thing is I don't feel any older inside. I still feel like I'm in my twenties until I take a good look in the mirror. I like to laugh. I like to play games (especially if I win!). I like to have sex. I like to play in the waves at the beach. I like dates with my girlfriend—by the way, she's also my wife. But I can't do some of the things I used to do. I'm not as strong physically. I have to be careful with my back and my left knee. I have issues with my heart that stem from my radiation treatments...or should I say my 1970s over-radiated treatments? Hey, they did the best they knew at the time and I'm still alive and kicking, so I can't complain. Jesus said he came so I could live life to the full. When I read that scripture, it's true at whatever age I read it. So, I'm living life to the full at sixty, and if I live to ninety I can still live life to the full because of Jesus. I've got a lot of things I want to do and accomplish if God gives me more time on this earth. I've got plans. I've got desires. I've got dreams—both kingdom and personal dreams. Would you believe me if I told you I wanted to write a murder mystery novel and have it on the best-seller list? Well, with whatever happens I'm kind of liking my future. I'm loving life now and I know I'll be loving my life then. Oh, and when (not if) I die, I know God's got an even better plan for me. WOW!

If you can learn to love the journey that you are on, you will begin to love yourself. Don't allow the regrets of the past, the problems of today, and the fears of the future to ruin the beautiful life God has given you! Make peace with your past, get strength from God for challenges of the present, and have faith for the future.

Will we ever love ourselves perfectly? Maybe not. Our fallen world creates holes in us that limit our capacity to love ourselves as we should, and we must continually work on our own healing. However, understanding the goal of loving ourselves makes us radically different in this world.

Kay: I remember times when my children were small and life seemed full of demands. Every day I eagerly looked forward to 5:30 in the afternoon when the children's television show Mr. Rogers came on. After the hustle and bustle of a busy day, I breathed a sigh of relief when he sang his song, "It's You I Like." I heard Mr. Rogers' melodious voice convincing me that he liked me, my feelings, my ups and my downs, whether old or new. Even as a grown up, I needed to hear those words. They reminded me of how God felt about me and how I could feel about myself! Now, several years later, I still need to be aware that feeling good about myself is OK. God's reassuring voice is the one I hear, letting me know that I can like myself, because he likes me too.

Embracing Love Secret 4 is imperative to living a life of love. If, and only if, you love yourself God's way then, and only then, can you love others God's way.

> **Love Yourself God's Way → Love Others God's Way**
> **Greater Love for Self *Allows* Greater Love for Others**
> **Lesser Love for Self *Allows* Lesser Love for Others**

LOVE SECRET 5

Obedient Love

How can you know if you really love God? Is it a feeling you get every day? Are you overcome with a sensation? Is it a happy emotion? Although those kinds of moods are often enjoyed if you have love for God, the proof of your love for him is obedience. Obedience to God is not just an obscure idea in the Scriptures. On the contrary, the theme of obedience is impossible to miss in the Bible. However, in many versions of Christianity today, obedience is minimized if not entirely tossed out.

A true Christian is one who has agreed to live a life of complete obedience to Jesus. A true Christian is one who says, "Jesus is Lord" and means it. A true Christian recognizes Jesus as the Master and has willingly become his slave. The concept of being a slave to Jesus was discussed in "Love Secret 3: Self-Denial Love," but now, in Love Secret 5, we will go deeper into the vital and sometimes shocking realization about what obedience means.

> **Lack of Obedience to God = Lack of Love for God**
> **Obedience to God = Love for God**

We should begin by reading some of the very straightforward scriptures combining love and obedience:

"If you love me, keep my commands." (John 14:15)

"Whoever has my commands and keeps them is the one who loves me. The one who loves me will be loved by my Father, and I too will love them and show myself to them." (John 14:21)

Jesus replied, "Anyone who loves me will obey my teaching. My Father will love them, and we will come to them and make our home with them." (John 14:23)

"Anyone who does not love me will not obey my teaching. These words you hear are not my own; they belong to the Father who sent me." (John 14:24)

"If you keep my commands, you will remain in my love, just as I have kept my Father's commands and remain in his love." (John 15:10)

This is how we know that we love the children of God: by loving God and carrying out his commands. (1 John 5:2)

We know we have come to know him if we obey his commands. The man who says, "I know him," but does not do what he commands is a liar, and the truth is not in him. But if anyone obeys his word, love for God is truly made complete in him. (1 John 2:3–5a)

And this is love: that we walk in obedience to his commands. (2 John 1:6a)

In fact, this is love for God: to keep his commands. (1 John 5:3)

With these verses in mind, let's look at three aspects of obedience:

1. A Relationship of Obedience
2. Maintained-by-Repentance Obedience
3. Perfect Obedience

A Relationship of Obedience

In the center of his powerful and eloquent Sermon on the Mount,

Jesus reveals a truth that is crucial to our understanding of obedience: *"No one can serve two masters"* (Matthew 6:24a). In the twenty-first century, we might easily contradict Jesus because of our view of a master. We would compare a master to an employer, and possibly argue, "Yes, I can serve two employers. I have two jobs and I do them both well!" But that claim is made with a lack of understanding about a master. As a paid employee, yes, you could possibly serve two employers. BUT if you are a slave, then that wouldn't work. A slave can only be owned by one master.

Slaves and masters. What do those words conjure up in your mind? Probably unpleasant thoughts. We don't like the idea of slavery. We would much prefer being compared to "children," or "brothers" or "branches" or even "sheep"! We call ourselves "Christians" or "disciples" or maybe "believers." Those words flow very easily off the lips. But the word "slave"? We bristle at that word, but maybe it's the one we should be using instead of any other! It would help us to better understand our relationship of obedience to Christ. What may help us is to remember, as was stated earlier in Love Secret 3, that Jesus took the mantle of slavery first:

> *[Jesus], being in very nature God,*
> *did not consider equality with God something to be used*
>   *to his own advantage;*
> *rather, he made himself nothing*
>   *by taking the very nature of a servant [slave],*
>   *being made in human likeness.*
> *And being found in appearance as a man,*
>   *he humbled himself*
>   *by becoming obedient to death—*
>   *even death on a cross!* (Philippians 2:6–8)

Our perfect example, Jesus, God in the flesh, took on the identity of a slave. He displayed humility and obedience. His obedience went so far as to be obedient to death.

> *Jesus gave them this answer: "Very truly I tell you, the Son can do nothing by himself; he can do only what he sees his Father doing, because whatever the Father does the*

Son also does." (John 5:19)

So Jesus said, *"When you have lifted up the Son of Man, then you will know that I am he and that I do nothing on my own but speak just what the Father has taught me."* (John 8:28)

"But he comes so that the world may learn that I love the Father and do exactly what my Father has commanded me." (John 14:31)

Jesus' whole life was centered on doing exactly what the Father told him to do. He was obedient in all things. Jesus gladly became a slave. As his followers, we too become slaves, and Jesus is now our one and only master. We can never take this aspect out of the Christian life! The word *kurios* in Greek means master, or lord; someone who is supreme in authority. It signifies the one who is the owner. As Christians, we proclaim that "Jesus is Lord." Our identity is in the fact that we have made Jesus our master in all things. When he invites us to follow him, he calls us to give up everything and take up the cross. Our lives are no longer our own. It's no longer about what we want or desire, but it's about what he desires. We are his slaves.

The hesitation today in using the word "slave" unfortunately obscures the meaning of true Christianity. People often speak of Jesus in a way that makes him comparable to a personal butler or a cosmic bellhop. We say jump and Jesus says, "How high?" Then, when things don't turn out the way we expected, disappointment and disillusionment set in.

But for those who embrace being a slave of Christ, who are ready to obey him in all things, the prize awaits! Jesus is a master filled with love, compassion and kindness. It is an honor and a privilege to serve him. The master wants what is best for us; in addition, he wants to make you his friend. The slave-master relationship must be established first, but that relationship expands as we become more aware of God's will. *"You are my friends if you do what I command. I no longer call you servants, because a servant does not know his master's business. Instead, I have called you friends, for everything that I learned from my Father I have made known to you"* (John 15:14–15).

Most slaves are not privy to the details of their master's business. But Jesus wants to include his followers in all that he has learned from the Father. We are slaves subject to incredible privileges because our master is Jesus Christ.

There is freedom in being a slave! We are no longer "enslaved" to sin. We are free to be obedient to Jesus. Being an obedient slave takes the guesswork out of our life of faith. If God says it, we don't argue or complain; we obey. The following story provides a good illustration:

A farmer sent his son out into a field to begin work on a fence. He told the son that there were four posts placed exactly where he wanted them to be, and the son needed to go set them in the ground. The son went out to begin work. He found the first post and agreed that it was in a good location, so he dug a hole and set the post in the ground. The second post was 1000 feet north of the first one. This made sense to the boy, so he set that one in the ground. The third post was 1000 feet west from the second. The boy began to see the fence taking shape and set that post in the ground. He had a hard time finding the fourth post. It wasn't where he had expected it to be to make a nice square fence. Instead it was 1350 feet south of the third post. This didn't make sense to the boy, so he moved it up a few hundred feet to make a perfectly square fence.

Did the son obey his father? You would probably agree that he did not obey him with regard to the fourth post, but maybe you think he did obey with the other three. But in actuality, the number of times the son obeyed was zero. Why? Because he only obeyed when he agreed! The son obeyed his own judgment with all four posts. His first three decisions just happened to agree with what the father wanted. It's not obedience to God when a choice of lifestyle just happens to agree with a command of God. Obedience must be when God's commands make sense and when they don't make sense to us. We must do his will, not ours. We make him happy, not ourselves. Again, we are to do this without reservation, question or argument. And now the rest of the story. What the son did not know was that he was fencing off his inheritance and the extra length on the one side would have included a gusher of an oil well!

Being a slave also takes away some of the self-focus that we all wrestle with. Life is simple: Jesus is Lord (Master). I am his slave. I'm owned by him. He's purchased me by his blood. He has redeemed me from the clutches of Satan. He provides for me, protects me and gives me a purpose. It might help us to regularly recite a verse from Psalm 100: *"It is he who has made us, and we are his."*

Let's return to our first question: How do you know if you really love God? Well, everyone would probably agree that the Apostle Paul loved God. How did he see himself? He identified himself as a slave (*doulos*) of Jesus (Romans 1:1). What about Peter and John? They too called themselves slaves of Jesus (Acts 4:29, 2 Peter 1:1). Paul included Timothy and Epaphras in the same description (Philippians 1:1, Colossians 4:12). Not to be outdone, James gave himself the title of slave also (James 1:1). Jude came along and introduced himself as James' brother, but first as a slave of Jesus Christ (Jude 1). These are all men who were devotedly, completely, wholeheartedly lovers of God. Their deep love was rooted in their obedience to their Master, Jesus.

Even the angels want to join us in being a slaves. In John's visions found in the book of Revelation, one of the angels told him, *"I am a fellow servant [doulos] with you and with your brothers and sisters who hold to the testimony of Jesus"* (Revelation 19:10). We are in exciting and glorious company as slaves of Jesus Christ!

RANDY: *Years ago, as a relatively young Christian, I read the book Call to Discipleship. One of the chapters was entitled "The Duty of a Servant." I don't remember all that much about the book except that I made a copy of pages 42 and 43. It has always helped me to remember the decision I made to become a slave/servant of Jesus. The reading (with a few tweaks) is talking about Jesus being the pearl of great price and that it is worth everything to have him. I share it here with you:*

> So when man finds Jesus, it costs him everything. Jesus has happiness, joy, peace, healing, security, eternity. Man marvels at such a pearl and says, "I want this pearl. How much does it cost?"

The seller says, "It's too dear, too costly."

"But how much?"

"Well, it's very expensive."

"Do you think I could buy it?"

"Oh, of course. Anybody can."

"But you say it's too expensive. How much is it?"

"It costs you everything you have—no more, no less—so anybody can buy it."

"I'll buy it."

"What do you have? Let's write it down."

"I have $100,000 in the bank."

"Good, $100,000. What else?"

"I have nothing more. That's all I have."

"Have you nothing more?'

"Well, I have some dollars here in my pocket."

"How many?"

"I'll see: 30, 40, 50, 80, 100, 120...120 dollars."

"That's fine. What else do you have?"

"I have nothing else. That's all."

"Where do you live?"

"I live in my house."

"The house too."

"Then you mean I must live in the garage?"

"Have you a garage, too? That too. What else?"

"Do you mean that I must live in my car, then?"

"Have you a car?"

"I have two."

"Both become mine. Both cars. What else?"

"Well, you have the house, the garage, the cars, the money, everything."

"What else?"

"I have nothing else."

"Are you alone in the world?"

"No, I have a wife, two children..."

"Your wife and your children too."

"Too?"

"Yes, everything you have. What else?"

> "I have nothing else; I have only myself."
>
> "Yourself too. Everything. Everything becomes mine: wife, children, house, garage, cars, money, clothing, everything. And you too. Now you can use all those things here, but don't forget they are mine, as you are. When I need you or any of the things you're using you must give them to me because now I am the owner."

Jesus is my master and I am his slave and he owns everything. He has treated me so much better than I deserve. He has given me so much to enjoy in this life even as I "own" none of it. He has instructed me in the wise and success-filled way to live with an outcome more grand and glorious than I ever expected. I wouldn't trade anything in the world for my Jesus!

Maintained-by-Repentance Obedience

We are taught from the Scriptures that every person must repent and make Jesus Lord at baptism (Acts 2:38; Romans 10:9). Baptism is a one-time event, but repentance is something that is ongoing in our Christian walk. In order to continue in obedience, we must continue in repentance. Again, we have a word that is often misunderstood and misapplied in the world today. Cartoons abound that depict ragged prophet types, wearing sackcloth and carrying a sign that says, "Repent—the end is near." When the word "repent" is heard, many people assume that the meaning has to do with feeling bad, and that it's a negative thing. But repentance is a positive thing! Repentance means to turn around, to change direction, and to turn toward something different. Repentance means we don't have to stay the same. We can change and live the lives we were created to live. We can turn away from wrong and head for what is right. The command to repent is a command of hope, telling us to turn toward God.

We have a perfect example of repentance and the indications of repentance in a letter written to the Corinthian church. After a scandalous incident occurred, the Christians had done their part to rectify a very bad situation. Although they were very sad and sorry about how they had mishandled the problem previously, their repentance produced joy:

Godly sorrow brings repentance that leads to salvation and leaves no regret, but worldly sorrow brings death. See what this godly sorrow has produced in you: what earnestness, what eagerness to clear yourselves, what indignation, what alarm, what longing, what concern, what readiness to see justice done. (2 Corinthians 7:10–11a)

This passage compares two types of sorrow over sin—worldly sorrow and godly sorrow. Worldly sorrow looks convincing. Those with worldly sorrow might be tearful and say all the right things. But worldly sorrow does not produce lasting change. Worldly sorrow is all about feeling embarrassed and "caught." Those with worldly sorrow are not too concerned about how God feels about a sin, or how their sin has hurt God or others. Worldly sorrow does not show love for God or appreciation for what Jesus has done to forgive their sins. So worldly sorrow is really worthless sorrow! Godly sorrow, on the other hand, does bring about a change. Notice that godly sorrow does not equal repentance, but it does bring about repentance.

Having godly sorrow that brings repentance is seen by the following indicators in your life:

1. **No regret**—You have no regret about giving up sin or a sinful lifestyle. Instead, you are thankful that you don't have to live in that sin any longer. You don't second-guess your choice to change, and you are determined that you won't go back to the way you were.

2. **Earnestness**—You took the matter seriously and no longer just shrugged your shoulders about a sinful situation. You responded immediately and welcomed the challenge without any resentment.

3. **Eagerness to clear yourself**—You had a full recognition of your responsibility and you dealt with it rapidly and completely. You didn't allow your heart to become hardened to sin. Like a stain on clothing, you knew it must be dealt with quickly.

4. **Indignation**—You weren't indignant with God or with someone who was trying to point you in the right direction, but you were indignant with how the sin was leading you astray. You were indignant that Satan tricked you. You were indignant that you allowed someone else to tempt you. The indignation makes you adamant about never allowing it to happen again.

5. **Alarm**—There was a proper sense of alarm about what sin can do to you. You realized that sin can become commonplace and acceptable. You see that you could become numb and hardened to sin. This gives you a healthy dose of fear of the power of evil.

6. **Longing**—Godly sorrow produced longing, affection and a strong desire for God and for the ones you have sinned against. You are drawn more to God in prayer and Bible study, and you appreciate God's forgiveness and grace more deeply. If there is someone who had to confront your sin, you realize the love it took for them to do so. Your affection for them deepens, knowing that they could have remained aloof or indifferent, but they were willing to speak up.

7. **Concern**—You did not address the sin with a lazy, half-hearted attitude, but with zeal. It stirred you up and produced in you a passion to *do* something! You weren't about to run out of energy before the matter was settled. You had the strength to continue until the issue was resolved.

8. **Readiness to see justice done**—You were willing to go through any unpleasant talks, confessions or changes to make sure that the process was complete. The only thing that mattered was repentance, and you were determined to get there!

To continue to live in obedience to Jesus, we must continue to live in repentance. Repentance is what brings us into times of refreshing from God (Acts 3:19). Repentance is the reminder that we are still growing, still changing and still loving God! None of us have arrived, but repentance keeps us going in the right direction as it cheers, revitalizes, renews, enlivens and breathes new life into us.

Perfect Obedience

Uh-oh...did we just say "perfect"? Didn't we already admit our need for a continual repentant attitude and for change? Then how is it that our love requires perfect obedience? There are so many wonderful paradoxes in our relationship with God, and this is one of them. We acknowledge our lack of perfection, our sins and our failures. We must do that, and we must remain humble. As a matter of fact, Jesus told a parable about the sinner who was exalted because *"he would not even look up to heaven, but beat his breast and said, 'God, have mercy on me, a sinner'"* (Luke 18:13). So how on earth can we claim that our love for God is based on perfect obedience?

You are right; none of us can claim perfection. But we can claim the One who is perfect, Jesus Christ. Having him as our Lord, Master and Savior makes us perfect in the sight of God. *"But if we walk in the light, as he is in the light, we have fellowship with one another, and the blood of Jesus, his Son, purifies us from all sin"* (1 John 1:7).

Because of the blood of Jesus that we initially came in contact with in baptism, we can boldly say: "I am perfect." It's certainly not because God has bad eyesight, but because he has provided a way for us to be perfect. Jesus' death on the cross solved the problem of sin once and for all. As we walk in the light (walk in obedience), the blood of Jesus is like an ever-flowing fountain that continually purifies us from all our sin. Whenever God looks at us, he sees us through the blood of his Son and sees us as perfect. So, by walking in the light, we will show our love for God and our appreciation for him by never taking for granted what he has done for us. Because of his grace, we want to live in obedience to him.

It's a mystery to see how some people can take that grace for granted and even abuse God's grace. But it's nothing new. *"For certain individuals whose condemnation was written about long ago have secretly slipped in among you. They are ungodly people, who pervert the grace of our God into a license for immorality and deny Jesus Christ our only Sovereign and Lord"* (Jude 4). These kinds of people live with the attitude that obedience is unimportant. But those who love God and are grateful for all he's done take a different stance:

> For the grace of God has appeared that offers salva-
> tion to all people. It teaches us to say "No" to ungodliness
> and worldly passions, and to live self-controlled, upright
> and godly lives in this present age, while we wait for the
> blessed hope—the appearing of the glory of our great God
> and Savior, Jesus Christ, who gave himself for us to redeem
> us from all wickedness and to purify for himself a people
> that are his very own, eager to do what is good.
> (Titus 2:11–14)

Let's return once more to our initial question. How can we know we love God? It's humorous how different types of people answer that question. There are some who are very confident and feel assured that their love for God is genuine. Then there are others who question themselves and wonder if they love God enough. We see in this that the answer is not in the feelings. The answer is in the obedience. We have a relationship of obedience as a slave of Jesus. Our obedience is maintained by repentance. And our obedience is perfect obedience—not because of our own perfection but because of the perfection of Christ. In the end this allows us to feel good about ourselves. When you do right, you feel right. That's just the way God made us to work. So loving God and demonstrating it through our obedience is the only way to live a fulfilled, satisfied, happy, content, cheerful and refreshing life. Sounds good, doesn't it? Love Secret 5 is: we can know we love God if we obey him.

> **Lack of Obedience to God = Lack of Love for God**
> **Obedience to God = Love for God**

LOVE SECRET 6

Discerning Love

God has made each person unique and wonderful and beautiful. Our individual fingerprints testify to the differences in every human being. We don't think alike. We don't look alike. We don't sound alike. We don't process things in the same ways. We don't have the same interests. We don't have the same talents. We don't have the same intellectual abilities. We don't have the same perspectives. We don't have the same dreams. We don't have the same weaknesses. We don't have the same strengths. We don't have the same color of eyes. We don't have the same color of skin. We don't have the same color of hair. For all these reasons, when it comes to effectively loving someone, a one-size-fits-all approach just doesn't work!

The fifth love secret is this: To the degree you effectively discern (figure out) a person, to that degree there will be an affective connection of love. We'll be looking at Love Secret 6 from the perspective of a scripture that is primarily about raising children correctly. But then we can expand on the principles and make it work with our interactions with all people.

Effective Discernment Produces Affective Love

The passage we want to concentrate on is Proverbs 22:6. It's a passage expressing how a parent is to love their child through training. As we consider it, also keep in mind the portion of Proverbs 13:24 that states *"the one who loves their children is careful to discipline them."* So training or discipline absolutely demonstrates love. This is an important and understandable concept whether you have children at this time in your life or not. Let's look at it in a number of translations.

Start children off on the way they should go,
and even when they are old they will not turn from it.
(Proverbs 22:6 NIV)

Train up a child in the way he should go,
Even when he is old he will not depart from it. (Proverbs 22:6 NASB)

Train children in the right way,
and when old, they will not stray. (Proverbs 22:6 NRSVA)

Most parents view their new baby as a soft lump of clay. They think the child is pliable in their hands. They think they can take the personality of their baby and squeeze it, roll it and mold it into any shape they want. Then they think they can pop it in a kiln (potter's oven) until it's good and hard. After that, they can send the child out to face the world. The problem with this thinking is that all clay is not the same. The properties of the different types of clay must be taken into account. The clay can be shaped, but only to the extent that the properties of the clay allow it to be shaped. The preestablished characteristics of the clay determine, to a large extent, how it can be shaped and how it will respond to the fires of the oven. And so with this in mind, the personality of the child can be *influenced* by the hands of the parents but the preestablished characteristics of the child determine how it can be molded and to what extent it can be molded.

Most people approach this scripture with a simplistic perspective, assuming that a child will turn out right if the parent does everything right. In other words, if you take the child to church and make sure that the Bible is read and scriptures are memorized, and if the child is always in a Christian type of atmosphere, then that child will remain on the straight and narrow path. The thinking continues with the idea that even if the child plays the prodigal and morally leaves the Father's house for a distant land, that at some point, they will come back to God. The problem with this idea is that real life tells us that all prodigals do not come home.

So what's the correct interpretation of Proverbs 22:6? We will discuss the definition, the duration, the delivery and the demonstration of the training. This will give us insight to loving our own children and other people in an effective manner that affects their lives in godly and positive ways.

Definition of the Training

The word "train" (or "train up") has two main ideas encapsulated in the meaning or definition of the word itself. The first use of the word is better understood when we learn that the root of the Hebrew word for "train" was used to describe the actions of a midwife after the birth of a baby. To "train" the baby, the midwife would rub her finger into the juice of crushed dates and then gently massage the infant's gums and palate. This tangy taste would create a sensation for sucking. After this, the midwife would put the baby into the arms of the mother for nursing. To "train" a child, a parent must create a thirst and an instinctive desire for the parents' nourishing flow of wisdom, knowledge and counsel.

The second use of the word was to "train" a wild horse by placing a rope in its mouth. This would bring it into submission. A wild horse is a thing of beauty and power, but it does no one any good until it is broken or under control. Then it can be guided and directed into usefulness and productivity. It is the same for every child. After all, no one likes an out-of-control kid! There is a certain amount of "wildness" in every child. They must be brought into submission in a right way to authorities, especially the authority of their parents and of their God so that their lives are useful and productive. With children there is to be the right use of discipline to bring about the right type of submission in behavior and the right type of submission in respect.

Now let's take what we have learned and apply it to loving people in general. Loving others includes providing an atmosphere that helps them in their spiritual walk. We hope to create and maintain within others a thirst for God's wisdom, knowledge and counsel. It would be unwise to assume someone has the desire for God and treat them as if they did. The whole purpose of the relationship would be altered.

Let's say a physical trainer offers a potential client a great gym membership and an awesome workout plan. But the client is not hungry for physical training. He is not motivated to use the membership or follow the workout schedule. Only when the client has a desire for the training will he appreciate it. Pointing out the many benefits of physical training such as becoming healthier, living longer, looking better and feeling better would all help to create a thirst, a hunger, a desire to train at a gym. Obviously the "workout" plan for the Christian is the Bible. We love by inspiring each other to remain faithful to God and to his word. *"Let your conversation be always full of grace, seasoned with salt"* (Colossians 4:6). Having conversations that are "seasoned with salt" develops a thirst in others for what is most important in life.

Duration of the Training

"Train up a child." This passage specifically uses the word "child." Often we think of a child only being one who is in the first few years of life. Yet we find the Scriptures using the same Hebrew word in a broader sense—from infancy to a young man of marriageable age. The training principle applies to any dependent child living under the parent's roof:

1 Samuel 4:21	a newborn infant
Exodus 2:2–3	3-month-old Moses
1 Samuel 1:22	Samuel before he was weaned
Genesis 21:12–20	Ishmael as a preteen
Genesis 37:2	Joseph at age 17
Genesis 34:19	used of a boy of marriageable age

How does this help my love to be effective with my brothers and sisters in Christ? How can my love affect others in a good and positive way so that there is a good outcome to their lives? We certainly should not treat adults as children, but people are at different stages of spiritual maturity. The new Christian is a babe in Christ and will need much more specific attention, protection and help than someone who has been around for many years. The young Christian needs to be taught and needs to learn all the basics of Christianity, both the doctrines and the lifestyle. Of course, there is never a time a person doesn't need people in their lives to love them. Jesus said we must all become like little children. Isn't an aspect of being childlike being teachable? So regardless of age, to love others we must develop an atmosphere of learning, teaching and training one another.

Even in physical families, as we move from parent-to-child

relationships to adult-to-adult relationships, we want to continue to have this kind of atmosphere. As parents, we are always willing to help and remain involved in our children's lives even though they are grown up and have families of their own. It's the same way in a spiritual family.

On a similar note, it should be made clear that parents will remain the main spiritual influence in the lives of children who are living at home, even those who have made the decision to become Christians. Some parents give in to the thinking that others (ministry personnel or volunteers) will take over once their kids reach a certain age. Those outside of the physical family who help with these kids are a blessing, but the parents must remain engaged and involved! Similarly, the ones to help bring a person to Christ need to be the people who stay committed to helping raise that person up in Christ—he or she needs spiritual parenting.

Delivery of the Training

The delivery of training is suggested by the words *"in the way he should go."* This means "in keeping with" or "in cooperation with" or "in accordance to something." The literal rendering would be "according to his way." This is very different from according to *your* way, or *your* plan or *your* curriculum. It means that if you want your training to positively affect the life of your child, you must be observant and discover your child's way. In the vernacular of today, you have to "get" him or her. Then, you are to adapt your training accordingly. Even educators today are saying different kids learn and connect in different ways. A one-size-fits-all approach just doesn't work best in the classroom. A parent always appreciates the teacher who figures out the most effective learning way for their child. Parents are to have an attitude of adaption with each child. They are to carefully study an individual's character and capacity with a thoughtful concern to their future course in life. They are to watch for a child's natural inclinations. They are to consider the child's nature, faculties and temperament. Then the training and education can be tailored to the child's way, and in so doing, affect the child for a lifetime.

Too often we see parents who think they have their child's future figured out without having their child figured out. For example, a father who is an athlete and wants his son to also excel and love sports never quite connects to his son because the son has an interest in music or the arts. And because of this, he never really connects on the many more important aspects of life.

Let's continue to look at the words and concept of "training in their way." The same word "way" is used in Proverbs 30:18–19:

> *There are three things that are too amazing for me,*
> *four that I do not understand:*
> *the way of an eagle in the sky,*
> *the way of a snake on a rock,*
> *the way of a ship on the high seas,*
> *and the way of a man with a young woman.*

The Hebrew term for "way" literally means "road" or "path." Therefore, in a figurative sense it can mean "characteristic." The way, or what is preformed in an eagle to fly, becomes what is characteristic of an eagle. The way, or what is preformed in a snake to move on a rock, becomes what is characteristic of a snake. The way, or what is predetermined for a ship to float, becomes what is characteristic of a ship. The way, or what is prewired emotionally in a man, is characteristic of a man in love. So the idea here is that each child has characteristics that are preformed or predetermined or prewired by God. Every child is unique and has a distinct set of characteristics.

When talking about this concept in children, sometimes it is referred to as having certain "bents." This describes perfectly the concept we are emphasizing. Each child is not a totally pliable lump of clay. Each has certain bents prescribed according to a predetermined pattern. The word "way" also has to do with setting your foot on territory or objects. In Psalm 7:12, the word is used of God who *"will bend and string his bow"* or *"has bent his bow and made it ready."* In other words, God has set his foot on the bow in order to bend it and string it. In a similar way, God puts his foot on the physical, psychological and personality bows (bents) of our lives to bend them in specific ways. So these bents greatly affect how the child should be handled and how moldable the child will be.

Each child is unique. Each mind is intricately woven with the finest of neurological threads. Each child's emotions are unique. Each child's personality is unique. Just like snowflakes and fingerprints, no two are alike. Consider the radical differences of the following sets of brothers: Cain and Abel; Solomon and Absalom; Jacob and Esau. The last pair were even twins, yet they had such physical and psychological differences. Now consider your kids. How different are they? How distinct are they physically, mentally, emotionally and spiritually? You need to know your kids and appreciate what is unique about them. Then you need to train them according to their specific characteristics. Parents must understand and appreciate how fearfully and wonderfully each child is made!

Please remember that our primary goal is not to teach about child-raising. Our goal is to teach about love. We want you to know that the understanding of how to love/train/help/befriend a child is the same understanding needed to effectively love/train/help/befriend all people. Observe them. Figure them out. Who are they in their emotional makeup? What have they gone through and experienced in life? What has made them who they are today? What are their bents? Then you can love them their way, the way they can feel love and grow and flourish. We can't just do what worked to help us grow and mature. What a huge mistake it is to think everyone can be loved/trained/helped in the same way. We must love and train them in *their* way.

This would mean working with a person at their faith level, not at ours. It would mean knowing if they are an introvert or an extravert. It would mean being aware of the major hurts and pains in their lives. Some people thrive on being challenged, while others cringe at the same challenges. Some people are labeled in the psychological world as being HSP or Highly Sensitive People. Some people need more encouragement than others, often due to how they were raised. If we don't understand whom we are working with, it would be possible to inadvertently push them out the door of God's kingdom. It could mean that they don't receive the kind of love and patience and encouragement that we all need to receive to keep us going in the right direction.

RANDY: Believe it or not, by definition, I am an introvert. For me that means I need some alone time and quiet time to power up to be able to keep giving. The extravert, on the other hand, is powered up by being around people. Now, don't get me wrong—I love people, but I have had to learn to give and to keep on giving to people. I was not a person who enjoyed hanging out in crowds of people before I became a disciple. I had to learn to like fellowship and I had to learn how to fellowship. I actually ran away from it at the beginning of my Christian life. Also, I am at my core timid and shy. I even care too much about what people think about me. This has always made evangelism challenging for me. If I had been taught in my early years that Christianity was just about evangelism and that my effectiveness in evangelism is all that really counts, I doubt I would have made it as a Christian. I would have hated that kind of wrongly focused Christianity and thought I was a pretty big failure at it compared to some who were quite awesome. I always knew I needed to share my faith and I was always willing to try, but I was allowed to work according to my faith and not have to work according to others' faith who were further ahead in this aspect of being a disciple. Yes, all are to be evangelistic to be a true Christian. All are to become effective teachers to bring people to Christ. But this expectation and standard is to be trained with a sensitive understanding of who people are and with patience. I will always be thankful for the people who expected the best from me while treating me with love and respect.

KAY: *I am an HSP—a Highly Sensitive Person. This is also called Sensory-Processing Sensitivity. The definition of an HSP is not that the person is emotional or easily hurt, although that could be the case. It has more to do with how things are perceived and how a person deals with external influences. For me, I am uncomfortable in settings where there is a lot of noise or a lot of people. What does that sound like? Yes, it sounds like fellowship! I am easily distracted by movements or sounds, which make it hard for me to concentrate. I am also very aware of the body language and facial expressions of others, although I never claim that I am accurate in my assumptions about what someone is thinking! So, if someone wants to have a good conversation with me in the midst of a crowded auditorium, they may find me less attentive than they would like. But they will find me very interested and engaged if we are speaking one-on-one in a less chaotic atmosphere. If someone who knows me wants to be my friend, they wouldn't take me to a concert or a huge shopping mall on Black Friday. They would take me for a walk in the woods or to have tea in a cozy shop!*

Just so it's clear, it's never OK to say no to God in anything he commands, even when it is difficult for us. We must never use our own personality bents as an excuse for indifference. But as we understand ourselves better, we also see the importance of seeing others clearly so that we can effectively love them. For example, in any church membership, about half the people might be on the introvert side of life. As we focus on our mission to *"seek and to save the lost,"* the introvert might feel that that they never do enough when compared to the extravert. The truth could very well be that the "little" the introvert does has taken more trust in God and more courage than the "much" the extravert does. But does the "little" the introvert accomplishes receive the same kind of recognition and encouragement? They should receive even more!

A wonderful example of understanding that people are different is contained in the book *The Five Love Languages,* by Dr. Gary Chapman. In it he explains that we tend to try to love people the way we feel loved, yet people feel loved in five different ways. If you fail to love a person in their love language, they will not feel fully loved by you. The problem is compared to people speaking different languages that the other doesn't understand. They may be speaking to each other, but they are not really connecting. The book goes on to explain that most people have a primary love language and a secondary love language. The five love languages are: physical touch, receiving gifts, words of affirmation, quality time and acts of service. This demonstrates the need to pay close attention, to observe and then figure out who a person is. Then love them their way.

RANDY: Years ago, Kay and I went on a personal three-day marriage retreat. We took the book The Five Love Languages and read a portion each day and then discussed it. At the end, we asked each other the question, "What is your primary love language?" Although we had been married for about twenty years, I was shocked to learn Kay's love language was receiving gifts. Who knew? I needed to pay closer attention! It's been a great thing to understand for the past twenty years!

KAY: At the risk of sounding defensive, I'd like to defend my "love language" so that I don't appear too terribly materialistic! For me, receiving gifts is truly about "It's the thought that counts." It's not that the actual gift makes me feel loved. Rather, the love is felt because when I receive a gift, that giver is saying, "I've been thinking of you. In fact, I was thinking of you when I wasn't with you, and this trinket is proof of that!"

Another important passage of Scripture that we would like to add to these thoughts of loving a person their way is found in Matthew 7:12: *"So in everything, do to others what you would have them do to you for this sums up the Law and the Prophets."* What incredible words! Now, Jesus was not the first to say similar things. Man on his own can stumble over a truth that makes sense in life.

"Do not to others what you would not wish done to yourself."   —Confucius

"Do not do to anyone what you yourself would hate."
—Old Testament Apocrypha

The following is what Rabbi Hillel stated in 20 BC when asked by a would-be convert to teach him the whole law while standing on one leg.

"What is hateful to you, do not do to anyone else. This is the whole law; all else is only commentary." —Hillel

While the Golden Rule concept did not originate with Jesus, he refined it. As in so many teachings, Jesus was setting in order what humans had gotten out of order. Jesus was the first to state this great concept in a positive way. All the others said "don't." Jesus said "do." This focuses on activity, not passivity. So what are we to do if we are to love someone? We must have consideration of the one we are trying to show love to. We are to use our minds and creativity to figure out an individual. People want to be understood. People are drawn to those who discover what appeals to them...their likes and dislikes. In context, the Golden Rule scripture is placed next to a story about a father giving his son what he needs. People feel loved when their felt needs are met. People feel loved when others take the initiative to be involved, in the way they would like to be helped. For instance, some people want folks to visit them when they are sick and not feeling well. This helps them. Others (like Randy) just want to pull the covers over their head in a quiet room and ride it out with some chicken noodle soup (Jewish penicillin). We must love people their way!

Demonstration of the Training

Let's return to the scripture on training in Proverbs: *"When he is old, he will not depart from it...will not stray from it...will not turn from it."* The child who has been trained in *his* way by parents who have modeled the teachings by their own conduct and lifestyle is the child who will embrace what he has learned as he leaves home and is away from parental love, authority, discipline and example. Because of parents having effective discernment about their child, they can now see the demonstration or outcome of their training. Their love becomes affective or fruitful as the grown child (adult) thinks and behaves according to his training, especially in his relationship with God.

The Hebrew word for "old" in this passage means to be or to become old. Therefore, it could be suggesting someone approaching adulthood more than approaching retirement. We believe Solomon had in mind more a boy who was becoming a man than a sixty-year-old prodigal returning home. When the child reaches maturity, he will not depart from the way in which he has been trained.

What an incredible and true observation being made for all people for all time. But be aware that Proverbs 22:6 is not an absolute *promise* being made for all people for all time, because people ultimately have individual choice. Parents who have lived out this proverb cannot be continually blaming themselves if their child does not become a Christian or does not remain one. Certainly it would be right to consider what could have been done better or more completely, but the truth is we have all fallen short of being perfect parents. However, the proverb is an overall and absolute true observation of life...train a child in his way and he will not leave it when he grows up and is on his own!

What have we learned from this awesome passage of Scripture? That we are to observe with diligence and stay in touch with what the child is going through and experiencing. We should be looking to see how the child responds to different life situations. Children are always making themselves known, but the parent needs to put the time and concentration in to be aware. As we keep learning who our child is, we need to adapt and formulate our training to his way of embracing it. Our love and training must be done in a way that connects, is positive and is overall enjoyable.

RANDY: I am always so very thankful to God for giving me Kay as my wife. She has been a great mother to our two children. She was the one who was always more in touch with what they were feeling and going through. I would regularly ask and rely upon her sensitivity (and still do) to give me insight and to help me know the best way to love, train and connect to each child. We all need some outside-of-ourselves kind of help! By the way, Kay helps me to know how I'm making people feel in my preaching and teaching and personal interactions. She helps me to be better aware of what the people around me are feeling as they are going through this challenging thing we call life. I have to say that I don't always appreciate all input (my pride) but I know it helps me to love the people around me better.

We need to take these principles and practices learned from this child-raising scripture and put them into practice with everyone around us. A child is to be loved and feel loved. Our brothers and sisters need to be loved and feel loved. The church is a family. It's not a nuclear family, but still it is family and should be treated as such. We must observe each other with diligence. We must be in touch with what people are going through and dealing with...both the challenges and the joys. We are to train in such a way that they gladly embrace it and then keep it. It is to become a part of who they are. We are to study the people we are striving to love. We are to figure out who they are. What has a person experienced? What is their background? What are their triumphs, hurts and disappointments? How have they responded to different life issues? We must figure out how to best approach them so they will listen and learn. We have to be examples of what we teach. We need to consider what best motivates a person. We have to be good at getting to a person's heart.

And so Love Secret 6 is...

Effective Discernment Produces Affective Love

LOVE SECRET 7

Acceptance Love

Sometimes the simplest things are misunderstood. Several years ago our church was collecting a special donation for a leper colony in India. Every week the announcement was made to remember to put aside some funds for this leper colony. "Don't forget our special contribution coming up to raise money for the leper colony!" Finally the day came. A young boy had his money saved up and he was ready to give. His parents were pleased and asked him, "Son, tell us what we're collecting money for today." The boy proudly replied: "We're going to give to the leprechauns, of course!"

Another slight mistake in comprehension was realized when some church members, hearing the song "God Almighty Reigns," wondered for quite some time why they were singing that God "rains." Hearing the same song, there was one who thought he was singing: "the God of the mighty rings." (Watching too many *Lord of the Rings* movies maybe?) The things that some consider easy to understand can quite innocently be taken another way. Clear communication is everything! This brings us to the subject of this chapter, and the meaning of the word "acceptance." Truly, acceptance is a key in love, and it is Love Secret 7: As a person provides acceptance, a person provides love. But what is acceptance? A character in the movie *The Princess Bride* comes to mind. Inigo Montoya, hearing the villain use the same word incorrectly over and over finally says, "You keep using that word. I do not think it means what you think it means!"

It has already been made clear from previous love secrets that sin is unacceptable to God. So "Acceptance Love" is certainly not going to be about accepting sin or sinful behavior. Let's look first of all at one of the main scriptures that will direct our thoughts about this topic: *"Accept one another, then, just as Christ accepted you, in order to bring praise to God"* (Romans 15:7).

We will be looking at the context of this scripture later in this chapter, but let's start with the simple, basic principle. Christ has accepted you in order to bring praise to God! Everything about you has been received by Christ. No part of you is held back. Jesus doesn't label you, compartmentalize you or pigeonhole you. Your personality, quirks, temperament and baggage are all acceptable to God, through Jesus Christ. It doesn't matter what your love language is. It doesn't matter if you are a melancholy, a sanguine, a phlegmatic or a choleric. You can be an HSP, an introvert, an extrovert or an ambivert. You can be an ESF or an INT. As the song goes, "All of [God] loves all of you, loves your curves and all your edges, all your perfect imperfections." It's so freeing to know that Jesus doesn't categorize us in ways that we sometimes categorize ourselves. He sees you as a complete and whole human being with your own memories, issues and challenges. Jesus wants ALL OF YOU to be accepted by God, to bring God praise. When you grasp the meaning of Christ's acceptance of you, you will have the potential to extend that acceptance to others. You will be able to love in radical ways like never before!

Jesus gave very clear direction about how we should treat others who are in a different situation than our own:

> "Do not judge, or you too will be judged. For in the same way you judge others, you will be judged, and with the measure you use, it will be measured to you.
> "Why do you look at the speck of sawdust in your brother's eye and pay no attention to the plank in your own eye? How can you say to your brother, 'Let me take the speck out of your eye,' when all the time there is a plank in your own eye? You hypocrite, first take the plank out of your own eye, and then you will see clearly to remove the speck from your brother's eye." (Matthew 7:1–5)

The instructions are clear, and Jesus really means this. The human tendency in all of us is to find something about another person that we don't like or is very different from us. We look at the externals and form a critical opinion. It's also our tendency to jump to inaccurate conclusions and to label people. Then we go on to share our opinions with others. This creates a never-ending cycle of judgment. Why does Jesus speak so strongly about this? Because we are never able to know all the facts about another human being. We can't possibly know all the hidden motives behind their actions. Jesus goes on to caution us that in our judgments of others, we will receive the same kind of treatment. If we are insensitive and harsh in our judgment of others, then that kind of assessment will most likely be returned to us. But if we are gracious and merciful and forgiving, we can usually expect that in return.

Jesus even used a bit of exaggerated humor in this illustration. A "speck" is a little, irritating particle that is so tiny it's almost imperceptible. A "log" refers to a beam of timber. The contrast is bizarre enough to qualify for a *Far Side* cartoon. How can you remove a little piece of dust from another person's eye while you have a plank in your own? Notice, though, that Jesus never forbids trying to remove the speck, but rather forbids removing the speck without first dealing with the problems in your own eye.

Sadly, this is a passage that has been terribly misunderstood and misapplied. It seems that although there are many who don't know very much about the Bible at all, they do seem to know this one verse and quote it quite vehemently: "Don't judge me!" Unfortunately, the interpretation of the scripture is taken to mean that no one should ever try to "remove the speck."

The word "judge" is from the Greek word *krino*. It means to condemn, punish, avenge, conclude or to judge. In context, Jesus is condemning a hypocritical judgment of another. Jesus does not forbid a judgment between truth and error, nor does he forbid the ability to use discernment. Interestingly, the next statement out of Jesus' mouth calls for the ability to distinguish between what is sacred and what is not. *"Do not throw your pearls to pigs"* (verse 6). A little later Jesus teaches to judge between false prophets and true prophets: *"Watch out for false prophets. They come to you in sheep's clothing, but inwardly they are ferocious wolves"* (verse 15). Jesus clarifies the whole subject of judgment by these words: *"Stop judging by mere appearances, but instead judge correctly"* (John 7:24).

The problem we face is our tendency to make quick and impulsive judgments about the actions of others. We have never "walked a mile in their shoes" and can't understand certain behaviors. This is what Jesus is dealing with in his statement of *"do not judge."* This is what we must learn in order to have acceptance love. A simple example of this might be found in the parking lot of a hospital. You are driving behind someone who is moving so-o-o slowly. They seem to be deciding between parking and not parking. You are in a hurry and you become frustrated with the driver. You tap your horn; you get close to their bumper. Finally they pull over and let you pass. As you rev your engine to show your exasperation, you glance at the driver. You realize that he is someone you know! It's the neighbor whose wife is dying of cancer. She's a patient at the hospital and is facing her last days. You realize at this point that the driver is flustered, frightened and confused. Your judgment of him as just an indecisive and poor driver changes quickly to a judgment of concern, sympathy and understanding. You remember the meaningful quote: "Be kinder than necessary; everyone is fighting some kind of battle."

Another problem with hypocritical or disproportionate judgment is that it can become addictive. It's so easy to develop a habit of looking at others with a critical eye. We can become very quick to assume the worst instead of assuming the best. Our brains become wired to see everything that's wrong with a person instead of seeing everything that's right. This habit is destructive, not only for the one who is being judged but for the one who judges. It's a terrible and pathetic way to live life.

But we can't walk away from this passage without learning how to apply judgment from a proper, loving, biblical perspective. After all, Jesus did say to remove the speck. To be able to judge between truth and error is a mark of maturity. This is NOT what Jesus is prohibiting. We would be misapplying his words if we assumed we are never to get involved in teaching or correcting another person. Jesus is not telling us to turn a blind eye to sin or to suspend our discerning abilities. As the early church father Chrysostom wrote, "Correct him, but not as a foe, nor as an adversary exacting a penalty, but as a physician providing medicines." Here are some things to keep in mind when you see the speck in someone's eye:

1. To remove the speck, make sure your own hands and heart are clean. Examine yourself before you examine anyone else. In fact, be more thorough and stringent with

yourself than you are with someone else.

2. Specks make the eye tender, so be sensitive, careful and gentle. Try to be aware of the other person's struggles, background and circumstances. While these things are not excuses for sin, they are certainly helpful in explaining sinful actions.

3. Remember you are dealing with a precious soul that God loves dearly. The goal is never to prolong pain or to crush someone, but to bring them to a place of healing.

4. Once the "speck" has been removed, don't harp on it. Let it go. Don't make a person feel ashamed. The person will be in a vulnerable place; make sure they feel safe with you and free from accusation.

We will discuss the subject of restoring a sinner and the teaching about church discipline in the next chapter, "Love Secret 8: Tough Love."

Let's return to the context of the passage in Romans 14: *"Accept one another."* The letter written to the church in Rome reveals that there were challenges among the Christians about matters of faith versus matters of opinion. Just a few chapters earlier, Paul reminded the disciples:

> *Therefore, I urge you, brothers and sisters, in view of God's mercy, to offer your bodies as a living sacrifice, holy and pleasing to God—this is your true and proper worship. Do not conform to the pattern of this world, but be transformed by the renewing of your mind. Then you will be able to test and approve what God's will is—his good, pleasing and perfect will.* (Romans 12:1–2)

His appeal was first and foremost that each person would be surrendered to Jesus. Then, they would be able to learn to act and react like Jesus. Only then would unity be built among the brothers and the sisters.

His instructions then moved on to the subject of resolving

differences of opinions about specific issues. In this case, he was dealing with the varying opinions about what kind of food to eat and what special days should or should not be honored. This was a particularly tricky situation because the early church brought together so many varying cultures with diverse traditions. These differences had become a source of tension. Over 2,000 years later, we can relate to the tension, if not to the specific differences. We may not have a problem about meat that may have been sacrificed to an idol, and we might not quarrel over certain Jewish holy days. But we might often have differences of opinions about:

- Drinking alcohol
- Dancing
- Dress
- Watching certain movies or television shows
- Perceived materialism
- Halloween
- Politics

As we continue on this subject, we must remember that some issues are not a matter of personal opinion. Although this list is far from being exhaustive, it would include:

- The Bible is the Word of God.
- Jesus is the Son of God.
- A Christian is one who has faith in Jesus, has repented of their sins and made Jesus the Lord of their life, and has been baptized for the forgiveness of sins.

How did Paul deal with the challenges the Roman Christians faced? He instructed them to accept without condemnation. *"Accept the one whose faith is weak, without quarreling over disputable matters"* (Romans 14:1). He urged them not to treat anyone with contempt, because God has accepted them (verse 3). In fact, they were to stop passing judgment on each other (verse 13) and to make every effort to do what leads to peace and mutual edification (verse 19). His teaching went on to say that they could not bind something on another that was not demanded by God, but that they should be understanding of others' consciences and keenly aware of their own example. They were to treat others with respect and be willing to forsake anything that would hurt another person's faith (verse 21).

Although the circumstances were unique, the lessons are clear for us today. Let's say you consider yourself "strong" in the faith and can handle a cocktail or two before dinner. You don't get drunk, or even get a buzz, but you enjoy the taste. Nothing wrong with that. But if someone else, perhaps someone who is "weak" in the faith (a young Christian, or a person who struggles with alcoholism) sees this action, they might say, "Oh, he does it, so I can too!" And for them, it's a slippery slope because it violates their conscience and causes them to sin. But you stand on your rights. You don't want anyone to make you feel guilty for something that does not produce guilt in you. That may be allowable, but is it loving?

Accepting the one whose faith is "weak" would mean that you will refrain from drinking around that person. Or at the very least, you would make sure that your consumption of alcohol is not leading another person down the wrong path. You give up your right to drink in order to accept the one who might be damaged. You don't insist on exercising your liberty at the expense of another person's faith. That is just one example of acceptance love.

Ultimately, accepting another would mean that we must be understanding of differences without irritation, ridicule or contempt. But acceptance also goes a step further. We must enter the territory of the humble. To be accepting of others, there is no choice but to realize that "our way" is not always the only way. Our opinions, our perspectives, our viewpoints are just that: our own. When we are willing to see that our way of thinking is not the only way, then we are able to embrace and accept the way others think. In fact, we might even be moved to change our mind! But even if we don't, it's helpful to see other points of view. As the saying goes, if two people think alike all the time, one of them is unnecessary! Different perspectives and angles are helpful in solving problems, in creating dialogue, and in arriving at new and unexpected solutions.

KAY: *Randy and I have found that there are three little words that keep our marriage happy. You might think those three little words are "I love* *you." Those are certainly good words, and we do say them daily. But the three words I'm talking about are these: "In my opinion." We have learned not to be so dogmatic about the things we feel but to state our thoughts and then to add "...in my opinion." That helps both of us to realize that what we are thinking may or may not be totally accurate. It allows us to state our preference or feeling without it being a binding testament that can't be overturned. It keeps us both humble as we realize that our opinion may not be the best opinion, but it's still a valid opinion that needs to be heard. Try those three little words the next time you are in a "discussion" with a loved one!*

Jesus himself is again our perfect example in all things, including acceptance. Look at the men he chose to be with him! Among his chosen twelve were fishermen, a tax collector and a political zealot. The women who followed him were just as diverse and included one who had been demon possessed and one who was the wife of an important official in Herod's household. It's also clear that Jesus hung around all kinds of people, even those who were considered "undesirables." Children crowded around him. The sick and the sinful approached him. Clearly Jesus was a man who made others feel accepted. Of course Jesus challenged wrong behavior, but his love and acceptance made people rise to be all that he called them to be.

As we strive to become like Jesus, we will become more accepting, kind and gracious in our assessment and treatment of others. Critical judgment is a hard habit to break, but it can be done! Make a new habit of loving with acceptance. Here are some ways that can happen:

1. **Remain humble.** When you begin to protest, even in your thoughts, about someone else's behavior, opinion or way of doing something, remind yourself that your way isn't the only way. Remember that you don't have all the answers all the time. It's rather freeing to not have to defend yourself all the time. Humility can be very relaxing!

2. **Find the good.** Catch yourself in the act of criticism. Even if it's only in your mind, exchange the critical thought for a compliment of the person. Strive to look at the people

around you and notice something positive about each one. Of course, when you can, express it.

3. **Appreciate differences.** Realize that God made everyone unique and special. Instead of bemoaning the fact that someone doesn't see eye-to-eye with you, be aware that differences make for a fuller perspective. When you strongly disagree with someone, try to understand their point of view. As Stephen Covey says in his book *The Seven Habits of Highly Effective People:* "First seek to understand, then seek to be understood." Life will become richer when you are able to appreciate the vast array of outlooks there are in the world.

4. **Assume nothing.** Don't be quick to think you know why someone thinks a certain way or acts a certain way. Behavior is built on a range of assorted causes. Do you think you can really figure out someone so well that you know why they act like they do, without really asking or being involved in their life?

5. **Set an example.** Look at yourself first. Is the way you are behaving helpful to the other person? Before you criticize them, do you really have a better way?

6. **Pray.** If someone's actions are really troubling you, go to God with the situation. Often in prayer you will gain insight that will help your outlook.

Remember that loving someone will necessitate, at times, a need to address a sinful behavior or wrong thinking. But it's more likely that a person will feel accepted and safe if you take the previous steps first. When the time comes to correct or confront a sin, be discreet. Don't embarrass the person. Don't gossip. Speak in private. Tactfulness can go a long way. And finally, let God do his work. Allow him to work in the person's heart. You can't push someone to repent. It's up to them to make a change. Your job is done.

Choosing to love with acceptance is powerful. It brings power not only to the one you love but to yourself. There is freedom in letting people be who they are, without trying to make everyone like yourself. Think how boring life would be then! OK, maybe you still would like people to be like you. We accept you for that! But the truth is that when you are willing to accept, you are showing a strength that comes straight from the heart of God.

RANDY: When my son, Kent, was in eighth grade, he decided he wanted an earring. Although I knew it was "fashionable," this was something that I resisted. Later, when he was a senior in high school, he decided he wanted a tattoo. Both the earring and the tattoo were very hard for me to accept! But, my wife, along with a friend of ours who was an elder in the church, helped me to understand that, at that time, it was a way for kids to express themselves, and it certainly was a lot better than expressions through drugs, sex or alcohol! Later in life, Kent gave up the earring, but I have grown to accept, and like, the tattoo on his back: a Chinese symbol that means "God's messenger."

In the movie *Bridget Jones's Diary* (which we admit has some unacceptable aspects), Bridget is a woman craving acceptance. She'll do just about anything to get dashing, handsome Daniel to notice her. In the background of her life is stuffy Mark Darcy. Bridget's indifference to Mark is altered when he surprises her by confessing, "I like you just the way you are." When she repeats those words to her friends, they are astonished. "He likes you just the way you are?!" That statement completely changes her way of thinking. In the end (spoiler alert) Mark Darcy is the one she chooses, because he has chosen her, just the way she is.

Maybe on a better note, we can close this chapter with the words to a song that has moved many a heart. It exemplifies God's acceptance of us, and hopefully will help each of us to grasp the radical nature of Love Secret 7: as a person provides acceptance, a person provides love.

Provide Some Acceptance → Provide Some Love
Provide Total Acceptance → Provide Total Love
Provide No Acceptance → Provide No Love

JUST AS I AM

Charlotte Elliott, 1835

Just as I am, without one plea
But that Thy blood was shed for me
And that Thou bid'st me come to Thee,
Oh, Lamb of God, I come, I come.

Just as I am, and waiting not
To rid my soul of one dark blot,
To Thee whose blood can cleanse each spot,
O Lamb of God, I come, I come.

Just as I am though tossed about
With many a conflict, many a doubt,
With fears within and foes without,
Oh, Lamb of God, I come, I come.

Just as I am Thou wilt receive,
Wilt welcome, pardon, cleanse, relieve;
Because Your promise I believe,
Oh, Lamb of God, I come, I come.

Just as I am, Thy love unknown
Hath broken every barrier down;
Now, to be Thine, yea, Thine alone,
O Lamb of God, I come, I come.

LOVE SECRET 8

Tough Love

Consider your picture of success when it comes to love. Maybe you envision a couple happily married for many decades, growing old and walking hand in hand together through life. Perhaps your favorite image of love is a mother's love for her child. Another picture of successful love is two friends who are loyal to one another for a lifetime. On a larger scale, you envision a gathering of people from different backgrounds or nations being unified and helping one another. These are all perfect views of love. And they do occur in our world, if only we will stop and notice them. Love is all around us in many ways.

There are other views of love that, from one perspective, don't seem to be successful. Certain actions may not look or feel like love, at least from a human point of view. Love Secret 8 will deal with those seemingly unsuccessful pictures of love. "Tough love" is the decision to love in ways that could seem contradictory to all the things we've already learned. But tough love is always crucial in relationships and in the church. Tough love means taking actions that appear hurtful, but the end result and goal is to help and protect.

Jesus gave us an example of tough love in his interaction with a would-be follower:

> As Jesus started on his way, a man ran up to him and fell on his knees before him. "Good teacher," he asked, "what must I do to inherit eternal life?"
>
> "Why do you call me good?" Jesus answered. "No one is good—except God alone. You know the commandments: 'You shall not murder, you shall not commit adultery, you shall not steal, you shall not give false testimony, you shall not defraud, honor your father and mother.'"
>
> "Teacher," he declared, "all these I have kept since I was a boy."

Jesus looked at him and loved him. "One thing you lack," he said. "Go, sell everything you have and give to the poor, and you will have treasure in heaven. Then come, follow me."

At this the man's face fell. He went away sad, because he had great wealth. (Mark 10:17–22)

We know that Jesus, the perfect Son of God, was perfect in his love. When this rich man came and asked the "good" teacher the basic question of life, Jesus playfully told him who he really was by expressing that only God is "good." He had been unaware that by calling Jesus "good" he was calling him God! When Jesus recited God's commands, the man sincerely replied with the assertion that those commands were his code of living. Jesus' response was kind, but still shocking. If the man really wanted to have eternal life, there was only one way, and that was to follow Jesus. But for this man, it meant a great sacrifice of money and possessions. Obviously he had not considered that possibility and was unwilling to follow those steps. *"He went away sad."*

Did Jesus fail to love this man? Of course not; his love was successful, even though the choice that the man made was not. Jesus came full of grace (love) and truth (John 1:14). Authentic, genuine, real love is accompanied by truth. And the way we share the truth is the same as Jesus did with this man: he did it with love. In fact, we are commanded to speak the truth in love (Ephesians 4:15). Although the man's decision to walk away made him lose his relationship with Jesus, the love that Jesus had for him never changed. Additionally, the love was observed and noted by the disciples around him. It helped them to learn the lesson of love. Love has the highest standards, standards that must not be lowered even in the desire to have a relationship. And so, Love Secret 8 is:

The Absence of Tough Love Is the Absence of Real Love

In this chapter, we will deal with four aspects of "tough love":

1. Applying church discipline in cases of unrepentant sin
2. Dealing with cases of divisiveness and false teaching
3. Loving your enemies
4. Toxic love

Applying Church Discipline in Cases of an Unrepentant Sinner

In a book about radical love, there's no way around discussing the topic of church discipline. It's not our favorite subject, by any means. It's not a fun subject. But unless Christians and the church address it, not only will the subject be misunderstood, the passages in the Bible will be misapplied. This would lead to even more harm and less love. Church discipline involves formal correction of a person in the church who is stubbornly unwilling to repent of an obvious (biblically named) sin. Discipline of that person is practiced in order to protect the church and with anticipation that the sinner will change. The goal of any kind of discipline is always positive: the hope that the offender will be restored to the church and to his or her relationship with Christ. *"Brothers and sisters, if someone is caught in a sin, you who live by the Spirit should restore that person gently. But watch yourselves, or you also may be tempted"* (Galatians 6:1).

The word restore is from the Greek word *katartizo*, which means to repair, mend or restore. It's a word used for mending a fishing net or setting a broken bone. A public or formal form of church discipline always begins with that end in mind—the restoration of a sinner.

In situations that involve church discipline, there are often varying reactions:

1. **Sentimentality**—Because the church fellowship is close and loving, there are some who do not want to see any kind of discipline take place. Often with the best of hearts, they want to protect the person who is in sin. But they go about it in a way that is unbiblical, by being resistant to the direction of the Scriptures. In the same way, their attachment to the sinner causes them to be unable to see the harm that that person's sin will do to the church as a whole. They are blind to the consequences that the sin could potentially bring about. They may feel like the leadership of the church is unloving by their actions.

2. **Avoidance**—No one wants to confront the sin. It's hoped that the problem will clear itself up on its own.

3. **Hasty or misapplied discipline**—Unfortunately, there are times when a church leadership is either untrained or inexperienced in knowing how to apply discipline. Someone in the congregation is difficult or perhaps contentious, and the Scriptures and the person are handled poorly.

4. **Leaving no hope**—In some cases, the discipline is so severe that a person has no recourse but to leave and never return to the church. Instead of being extended a lifeline, the person is severed from any option of restoration.

Because none of those options are acceptable ones, it's crucial that we understand what the Scriptures say and what they do not say about church discipline. This is important for those who are serving in any position of leadership, and also for those who are not.

While the pattern for dealing with the process of church discipline can be varied, and different circumstances call for various strategies, Jesus gave an overall picture for applying discipline in church matters:

> *"If your brother or sister sins, go and point out their fault, just between the two of you. If they listen to you, you have won them over. But if they will not listen, take one or two others along, so that 'every matter may be established by the testimony of two or three witnesses.' If they still refuse to listen, tell it to the church; and if they refuse to listen even to the church, treat them as you would a pagan or a tax collector."* (Matthew 18:15–17)

In some translations, the wording used is "if your brother or sister *sins against you.*" More recent versions omit "against you." Either way, the process is the same. Jesus' instructions aim at resolution by first trying to win the sinner over by a private discussion. If he won't listen, take one or two others. That phrase bears a resemblance to one of the laws of the Old Testament: *"A matter must be established by the testimony of two or three witnesses"* (Deuteronomy 19:15).

Both of these preliminary measures show love and dignity to the person who is accused. First, a private and discreet conversation must take place. Second, an appeal is made by a small number of people who have in mind the best interest of the person involved. (Interestingly, the Old Testament passage that Jesus refers to seems to be dealing more with warning against unjust accusations without witnesses. It goes on to detail the punishment for someone who has accused someone else falsely.) If that course of action is not successful, the "church" is to be involved. Since the Greek word *ecclesia* (used here for "church") means the assembly of people who have been called out from the world to belong to God, we can assume that Jesus is suggesting a larger number of involved individuals. We can't specify exactly how large, but we can assume he would be referring to people who might be directly involved and know the offender. This process would absolutely call for the inclusion of the leadership of a congregation.

Finally, as a last resort, the unrepentant sinner would need to be avoided. Although this "feels" unloving, it is a protective measure for the other believers in many ways. The church community should be aware that although a sinner needs to be dealt with gently, long-term blatant and unrepentant sin must not be tolerated. Furthermore, this is a protective measure because it teaches Christians that righteousness cannot be legislated. Every person has to make their own decision about living for God and holiness. Love does not mean that we force this on anyone. If someone chooses to go down the path without Christ, the blessings of a church community will not be available to them. This loss of fellowship helps the unrepentant person to realize their sin is separating them from God. They can't have their sin and the fellowship too.

Probably the most extreme case of church discipline is found in Paul's letter to the church in Corinth:

I wrote to you in my letter not to associate with sexually immoral people—not at all meaning the people of this world who are immoral, or the greedy and swindlers, or idolaters. In that case you would have to leave this world. But now I am writing to you that you must not associate with anyone who claims to be a brother or sister but is sexually immoral or greedy, an idolater or slanderer, a drunkard or swindler. Do not even eat with such people.

What business is it of mine to judge those outside the

*church? Are you not to judge those inside? God will judge
those outside. "Expel the wicked person from among you."*
(1 Corinthians 5:9–13)

The bad news is that there was a church member in Corinth who
was having a sexual relationship with his stepmother (verse 1). Equal-
ly disturbing to Paul was the fact that the church in Corinth was simply tolerating the sin, excusing their lack of action by thinking they
were being loving in accepting sin. Everyone seemed to know about
this situation, and no one was doing anything about it. The good news
is in realizing that even the churches presented in the Bible were not
perfect! Problems and sins occurred just like in our present day and
age. In one sense, this should make us breathe a little easier. When we
deal with problems in our fellowship, we can know that we are not all
that unique.

Paul's admonition to the Corinthians is a reminder that it is only
those who have publicly committed to the lordship of Jesus that he is
dealing with in this situation. He sees that there are all kinds of situations outside of the church fellowship that we can acknowledge as
sinful. But those outside are living according to a different set of rules;
they have aligned with a different philosophy of life than ours. We
have no right to place our "judgment" on someone who never agreed
to carry the cross of Christ. Of course we will try to teach those people
about sin and righteousness, but if they choose not to accept the standards of God, it really does become none of our business. However,
when that sin seeps into the church, into the body of Christ, then Paul
is roaring mad! His instruction to the Corinthian church is to *"expel
the sinner."* With these words, Paul is referring to warnings that the Israelites received about false worship during the time of Moses. At that
time they were told that even if their own brother or child or *"the wife
you love, or your dearest friend"* was involved in the sin of idolatry,
they were deserving of severe punishment (Deuteronomy 13). Paul invoked the same principle with the Corinthians. The offending sinner
was not to be *"put to death,"* as it was with the Old Testament law,
but he was to suffer the consequences of his sin by having the church
fellowship withdrawn from him.

It is important to understand that the concept of withdrawal
of fellowship from brothers and sisters in Christ (the horizontal

relationships) is to demonstrate to the one who has sinned that he has broken fellowship with God (the vertical relationship) by continuing in the particular sin. After all, the horizontal relationships exist only because the vertical relationship exists. The hope would be that this would help them take their sin seriously as they lose the sweet fellowship with those they love and cherish. The desire is to help move them to godly sorrow and to repentance. It is also important to note that, in actuality, the person who persists in their sin is the one who is making the decision to cause the disfellowship. The discipline of withdrawing fellowship is simply a public recognition of the person's decision to rebel against God.

Later, it appears that the church in Corinth accepted and obeyed Paul's admonition. His next letter to the church there covers his feelings of concern over the church and his delight that they had abided by his instruction. Happily, it appears that the sinner in question has repented, and Paul's words reveal tenderness and mercy:

> If anyone has caused grief, he has not so much grieved me as he has grieved all of you to some extent—not to put it too severely. The punishment inflicted on him by the majority is sufficient. Now instead, you ought to forgive and comfort him, so that he will not be overwhelmed by excessive sorrow. I urge you, therefore, to reaffirm your love for him. (2 Corinthians 2:5–8)

As we have occasion (and hopefully very rarely) to be involved in any sort of formal church discipline, we must always remember the purpose: to remain obedient to God, to protect God's people, and to bring about a repentant heart in a sinner.

RANDY: *Dealing with people because of unrepentant sin is emotionally draining for everyone involved. Watching the shattered lives and broken hearts of those affected by the particular sin is very challenging. You hurt for the people who are hurting so badly. Being in church leadership for many years has brought me into a number of discipline situations. It's hard on the membership of a church even when everyone knows from the Scriptures it is the right and the loving thing to do. I have seen some who eventually repented and came back to God and to the fellowship of* *the church. I have seen some who have not yet returned, but the church was protected. There was one situation where a public disfellowship had to be administered. It was done in a respectful, prayerful and loving way. The church was sad in the right way. The church responded in the right way. The church took their own sin more seriously as it took this brother's sin seriously. The church followed through with the right actions. The thing I will never forget is how the church responded when this brother came back in full repentance after a period of time. Although the sin had been grievous, the acceptance back was glorious. It was the lost son parable coming true: "We had to celebrate and be glad, because this brother of yours was dead and is alive again; he was lost and is found." I am also reminded of a passage of scripture I memorized as a young Christian that is found in Isaiah 55:8–9:*

> *"'For my thoughts are not your thoughts,*
> *neither are your ways my ways,'*
> *declares the LORD.*
> *As the heavens are higher than the earth,*
> *so are my ways higher than your ways*
> *and my thoughts than your thoughts."*

It must be God's way and thoughts of love and not man's way and thoughts of love. God does know what he is doing!

To further accentuate the need to protect the church from danger, consider the apostle John's fiery and figurative message from Jesus to the church in Thyatira. Despite Jesus' commendation of love, faith, service and perseverance, he used scorching words about allowing sin to continue in their midst:

> *"Nevertheless, I have this against you: You tolerate that woman Jezebel, who calls herself a prophet. By her teaching she misleads my servants into sexual immorality and the eating of food sacrificed to idols. I have given her time to repent of her immorality, but she is unwilling. So I will cast her on a bed of suffering, and I will make those who commit adultery with her suffer intensely, unless they repent of her ways." (Revelation 2:20–22)*

There is no way that we can read these passages without complete agreement regarding the need to forcibly and conclusively address the problem of sin in the community of believers. It needs to happen in the right way, but it needs to happen! The motive, the process and the solution should all be done with love. In applying any kind of church discipline, it's good to remember these words: *"My brothers and sisters, if one of you should wander from the truth and someone should bring that person back, remember this: Whoever turns a sinner from the error of their way will save them from death and cover over a multitude of sins"* (James 5:19–20).

Dealing With Cases of Divisiveness and False Teaching

Hopefully you are convinced that loving action needs to be taken when matters arise that are unsettling to the church. Sometimes the ways in which those things manifest themselves are subtle, and other times they are obvious. The following scriptures could be understood as problems arising from within the church as well as from without:

> I urge you, brothers and sisters, to watch out for those who cause divisions and put obstacles in your way that are contrary to the teaching you have learned. Keep away from them. For such people are not serving our Lord Christ, but their own appetites. By smooth talk and flattery they deceive the minds of naive people. Everyone has heard about your obedience, so I rejoice because of you; but I want you to be wise about what is good, and innocent about what is evil. (Romans 16:17–19)

> Warn a divisive person once, and then warn them a second time. After that, have nothing to do with them. You may be sure that such people are warped and sinful; they are self-condemned. (Titus 3:10–11)

It's obvious that the kind of contentious and divisive actions described here are harming individuals in the church. Thus, the way to maintain a loving and faithful church was to reject the people who would potentially hurt others' faith. Obviously you can't disfellowship someone who is not in the fellowship to begin with. The discipline would have no meaning, therefore it could bring about no change. But you can warn the church not to be in fellowship (talk, dialogue, discussion) with a person who will harm or endanger their faith. As a child must be protected from the stranger ("Don't talk to strangers"), so the church must be protected from the divisive ("Don't talk to those who cause divisions").

The same thing seems to be occurring from within the church in Thessalonica, but this time the trouble is coming from a "believer."

> *In the name of the Lord Jesus Christ, we command you, brothers and sisters, to keep away from every believer who is idle and disruptive and does not live according to the teaching you received from us....*
>
> *Take special note of anyone who does not obey our instruction in this letter. Do not associate with them, in order that they may feel ashamed. Yet do not regard them as an enemy, but warn them as you would a fellow believer.*
> (2 Thessalonians 3:6, 14–15)

Each of these passages can be misconstrued if they are not read within their context, but the theme is still clear throughout. Someone who won't listen to reason, who won't change when appeals have been made, cannot continue to be a part of a church fellowship. Or, if they are not a part of the fellowship, they must be pointed out (marked) so that the church can be protected. Although it may seem obvious, these kinds of actions again require the involvement of congregational leadership. Be aware also that each scripture listed is not a one-size-fits-all template. These cases require much prayer and wisdom.

What does all this have to do with love? God loves the church enough to make sure that it is protected and nurtured. *"Christ loved the church and gave himself up for her to make her holy, cleansing her by the washing with water through the word, and to present her to himself as a radiant church, without stain or wrinkle or any other blemish, but holy and blameless"* (Ephesians 5:25–27). To keep the church as his beautiful bride, sometimes tough love is required.

Loving Your Enemies

Abraham Lincoln said, "Do I not destroy my enemies when I make them my friends?" That was a very politically astute insight! In life and in our real world, we can't always accomplish what Lincoln so boldly said, and in fact, neither could he. But we have an obligation, as we follow Jesus, to learn how to love our enemies as Jesus requires. This is another aspect of tough love because it's tough...on us!

> *"But I tell you, love your enemies and pray for those who persecute you, that you may be children of your Father in heaven. He causes his sun to rise on the evil and the good, and sends rain on the righteous and the unrighteous. If you love those who love you, what reward will you get? Are not even the tax collectors doing that? And if you greet only your own people, what are you doing more than others? Do not even pagans do that? Be perfect, therefore, as your heavenly Father is perfect."* (Matthew 5:44–48)

One of the very things that will make us stand out in this world as disciples of Jesus is the quality of loving those who don't love us back. Of course it's natural to love those who love us. But to be like our Father in heaven, we must strive to love those who give us no return, and in fact might even want to do us harm! Jesus compares the love of God to the sun, which shines on every person regardless of their behavior, and the rain, that falls on the good and the bad.

Love for your enemy certainly would necessitate the act of forgiveness, but goes a step further. To love an enemy involves doing something that will benefit them. It might be a quiet, private thing like prayer. It might be providing the enemy with some kind of help. Loving an enemy doesn't mean you agree with or approve of their actions. It is not a "touchy-feely" kind of love. In fact, the word Jesus used here was *agape*—the kind of love that is a decision of the will. This kind of love is what Jesus expects. We have examples of this kind of love recorded even long before the time of Christ: *"If you come across your enemy's ox or donkey wandering off, be sure to return it. If you see the donkey of someone who hates you fallen down under its load, do not leave it there; be sure you help them with it"* (Exodus 23:4–5).

This is an amazing passage, considering the Israelites' numerous complaints about their enemies! Furthermore, when the apostle Paul wrote to the Christians in Rome about loving their enemies (Romans

12:20), he was actually quoting from the proverbs of Solomon:

> *If your enemy is hungry, give him food to eat;*
> *if he is thirsty, give him water to drink.*
> *In doing this, you will heap burning coals on his head,*
> *and the LORD will reward you.* (Proverbs 25:21–22)

Whether the reference to "burning coals" is figurative or a reference to some symbolic gesture is uncertain. But the result is certain: when you choose to do good to an enemy, God will reward you. That reward might come in the form of a changed and repentant enemy, or it might not. Either way, a reward from God is promised.

KAY: When our daughter, Summer, was a kindergartner, she came home one day with a tearful tale. Some of the kids at school were being mean to her by calling her names and snubbing her. One of them, a prefigure to a Mean Girls character, was especially difficult. As a mom, it pained me to see my daughter bullied (but this was in the era before the word "bullying" made school principals go weak in the knees). However, I realized that it was a pivotal time to teach my daughter what it meant to follow Jesus. We read Jesus' words found in Matthew 5 and said a prayer together for the girl. Summer seemed to find comfort in this, and daily we made it a point to "pray for our enemy." I discovered that Summer made a little beaded bracelet to give to her! After a period of time, Summer announced that the girl was not being mean anymore, and in fact, although they weren't best buddies, they were getting along well. This process might have occurred with time anyway, but the lesson to Summer (and me) helped to forge the fact that our goal is to follow the words and actions of Jesus.

If we want to love radically, we must resolve to love our enemies, whomever they may be. An enemy could be your next door neighbor or someone from a nation across the globe. It could be someone of a different race or religion. It could be someone who hurts you, is mean to you or criticizes you. A person might be an enemy because of your faith. The response is the same. If we are committed to Jesus, we will be committed to loving and praying for our enemies.

Toxic Love

Finally, we must not leave the subject of tough love without dealing with one other area that is challenging for disciples. Although

Jesus calls you to turn the other cheek when you are mistreated (Matthew 5:39), he is not permitting you to willingly tolerate being abused. When you turn one cheek, the other is exposed. But after that one is exposed, you have no more "cheeks" left to turn. In fact, the only recourse is to turn around and walk away.

Forgiveness and love for your enemies must not be construed to mean remaining in a toxic environment. There are some situations that require a decision to remove yourself from a person who, by their manner or conversation, is depleting you spiritually or is harming you emotionally or physically. Remember, you must have enough love for yourself to enable you to love others. If someone is taking away your ability to care for yourself, then the righteous thing to do is to recognize it and deal with it accordingly. Sadly, there are too many people who go to one extreme or the other. They either make the person an enemy by seeking revenge or they allow themselves to be misused. Neither option is acceptable to God.

Let's be careful about one thing, though. The word "abuse" is broadly applied these days. If someone is in an abusive environment, it's a terrible thing and help must be offered through the church and through other sources. But let's not use the word lightly. If we use the word in a way that is not genuine, it is dismissive of those who are actually suffering from physical, sexual or verbal abuse. So, don't "abuse" the word by using it for situations that are not applicable.

"Tough love" is an important view of authentic, genuine, real love as defined by God. Tough love is a tough subject because there are so many variables and ways to deal with unique situations. The main thing that holds true in all of these settings is the heart to love as Jesus loves. Even when the results of tough love are not successful from our human point of view, it is always a success from God's point of view. Maintaining love to our enemies, to those who withdraw from us, and to those who oppose us creates a Christlike character. And being like Jesus is the greatest success of all!

Love Secret 8 is...

The Absence of Tough Love Is the Absence of Real Love

* NOTE FROM RANDY: Thanks to Roy Hession and his book *The Calvary Road* (published in 1950) for his thoughts and words found in Chapter 8 entitled "Are You Willing To Be A Servant?". Some of his phrases along with his preliminary points about a servant and his 5 marks of a servant have been used in this chapter. In the writing of this book, I used some of my hand written notes that dated back 35+ years. I recently discovered while reading *The Calvary Road* that I must have previously read it in the 1970s and used some of the servant points to help build a sermon. My apologies for not giving this credit at first.

LOVE SECRET 9

Sexual Love

There will be two possible ways people might deal with a chapter on sexual love:

- Person A will glance through the table of contents and see "Sexual Love." They will immediately skip all the other chapters and jump straight to this one. They want to read the racy parts!

- Person B will glance through the table of contents and see "Sexual Love." They will immediately decide that that's the chapter they won't read. They are afraid that it might lead them into temptation.

Whether you are person A or person B, or you are just turning the page and found yourself here, we want you to stay! This is an important chapter for everyone. Don't worry, it's not too racy. (Sorry for those who are disappointed!) But it will be truthful, specific, and hopefully helpful to all readers.

It would be ludicrous if a book on love did not include something about sex. It would be like saying, "Oh, let's talk about every aspect of love we can think of, but shhh—not sex!" Sex is like the elephant in the room; we know it's there but we don't really want to talk about it in mixed company. But God is not a prude and neither are Christians, or at least they should not be. This chapter is for those who are married, for those who are single, for teens and for the older folks. Everyone needs to be educated and instructed about sex. You can't turn on the television, open up your Internet browser or walk down the street without being bombarded with some idea about sex. It's blatantly all around us. It's talked about in school, at the office and on social media. Children are being instructed about sexual relationships starting in the third grade, if not sooner. And yet people are a little nervous about the subject being in a Christian book for all audiences! But unless we learn and teach the biblical and godly view of sex, then we are in danger of allowing ourselves and our children to be led into the worldly and secular realm of sexual confusion.

You'd think with all the experts and advice and blogs and therapists we'd have a better view of sex. But last time we checked, people are insecure on one hand and obsessed on the other. Pornography addiction brings incredibly destructive images into innocent minds and destructive expectations into marriage. People are messed up about sex! The problem is not with the sexual act itself, but with the distorted and consuming perspectives that plague so many. In this chapter, therefore, we want to give a clear and scriptural view of sex. We certainly won't be covering every aspect of the physical act, but we want to make sure that we portray sex in the way God intended. We'll start at the beginning, with Adam and Eve:

So God created mankind in his own image,
in the image of God he created them;
male and female he created them.
God blessed them and said to them, "Be fruitful and increase in number; fill the earth and subdue it." (Genesis 1:27–28a)

God saw all that he had made, and it was very good. (Genesis 1:31a)

Adam and his wife were both naked, and they felt no shame. (Genesis 2:25)

God created man and woman. They both bore God's image, which means that they both were to be God's representatives on this earth. But he created them distinctly male and distinctly female. Therefore, the sexual nature of man and woman are all part of God's design. Even anatomically, the joining of man and woman makes sense.

Adam and Eve lived in the garden together with no shame. Imagine that for a moment. What was it that made the Garden of Eden paradise? Was it the beautiful flowers and abundant fruit? Those things were pleasing, but what made it paradise was that they lived a life with no shame. They were free from feelings of embarrassment or disgrace. They never experienced guilt or humiliation. The sexual relationship was one that was in complete agreement with God's plan. Sex was not a bad word. Sex was never sinful. In fact, God had commanded them to *"fill the earth"* with their love.

Sex was created by God and had nothing to do with "the fall" of man. Some, out of ignorance of the Scriptures, have twisted sex into being the sinful temptation that brought about the curse of mankind. But as we look at the passages, we can clearly see that sex was a part of Adam and Eve's partnership before they were tempted by the serpent (Genesis 3). Of course the sexual act has to do with procreation, but God also created it to be pleasurable. Even the desires and longings we have are the result of the way God made each of us. With that in mind, we can be assured that sex is good. But it's only good within the boundaries for which God created it. This is so important because this is where so many people suffer due to our world's distortion of sex.

One of the most fundamental truths about sexual love is this: it's not for everyone! In other words, sex is NOT essential in order to have a full and happy life. Although every person needs to understand and appreciate God's view of sex, not every person will participate in it. Sex is designed to be shared between one man and one woman who are committed to one another in marriage. That's the only way sex will be enjoyed to its fullest extent, because that's the only way God planned it. God intended for sex to be enjoyed within the parameters of marriage. Sex outside of marriage damages and destroys authentic love. Those who are not married, either by choice or by circumstance, should never feel like they are being cheated out of something. It's a "love secret" in this book, but it's not *the* secret to love. Sex is good, but it's not everything!

> **Sex Is Good but It's Not Everything**
> **Sex Is Good but It's Not Essential**
> **Sex Is Good but It's Not for Everyone**

In this chapter we will be discussing the ways that sexual love can be an incredible joy and blessing within marriage. But before we get to the good news, we need to make sure we understand the bad news. Where has the human race gone wrong when it comes to sex? We won't be able to exhaust this topic; it's too big. But we can portray some of the problems that have made sex into a dirty word.

The Bible accounts do not cover up the ways that sex has been misused through the centuries. Marriage itself seemed to evolve from a monogamous relationship (faithfulness to one person) into polygamy (numerous marriage partners). Polygamy was not forbidden by God, although there were very specific boundaries provided, but Jesus made it clear that from the beginning, marriage was to be the joining of two people into "one flesh":

> *"Haven't you read," he replied, "that at the beginning the Creator 'made them male and female,' and said, 'For this reason a man will leave his father and mother and be united to his wife, and the two will become one flesh'? So they are no longer two, but one flesh. Therefore what God has joined together, let no one separate."* (Matthew 19:4–6)

One example of the problems of a polygamous marriage can be found in the family of Jacob. Jacob married Leah under a false pretense and later married the girl of his dreams, Rachel. To complicate matters further, there were two concubines in the mix. The jealousy and rivalry between the women could make for a fascinating reality television show. Here is the script for one episode, with Rachel and Leah bartering for the opportunity to have sex with Jacob:

> *During wheat harvest, Reuben went out into the fields and found some mandrake plants, which he brought to his mother Leah. Rachel said to Leah, "Please give me some of your son's mandrakes."*
>
> *But she said to her, "Wasn't it enough that you took away my husband? Will you take my son's mandrakes too?"*
>
> *"Very well," Rachel said, "he can sleep with you tonight in return for your son's mandrakes."*
>
> *So when Jacob came in from the fields that evening, Leah went out to meet him. "You must sleep with me," she said. "I have hired you with my son's mandrakes." So he slept with her that night.* (Genesis 30:14–16)

This passage doesn't even begin to delve into the problems between all the siblings. Jacob's family relationships were what we would call today highly dysfunctional. No wonder Jesus tried to clarify things for us!

From our perspective this may seem a bit comical, but now we move on to a subject that has no humor whatsoever. We have already mentioned (in "Love Secret 1: Destroying Love") the horrible event that occurred between David's son Amnon and his half-sister Tamar. But it bears repeating as we look at how the sexual desires of Amnon turned into the devastating act of rape. Amnon *"fell in love"* with Tamar and was *"obsessed"* with her. On his pretense of being ill, she came to bring him some food:

> But when she took it to him to eat, he grabbed her and said, "Come to bed with me, my sister."
>
> "No, my brother!" she said to him. "Don't force me! Such a thing should not be done in Israel! Don't do this wicked thing. What about me? Where could I get rid of my disgrace? And what about you? You would be like one of the wicked fools in Israel. Please speak to the king; he will not keep me from being married to you." But he refused to listen to her, and since he was stronger than she, he raped her.
>
> Then Amnon hated her with intense hatred. In fact, he hated her more than he had loved her. (2 Samuel 13:11–15a)

Tamar reasoned with Amnon, pleaded with him, and used the word "no." Her words fell on deaf ears. Amnon's desire for Tamar had nothing to do with loving her. He wanted to possess her, to have power over her and to use her for sexual release. Sadly, events like this occur daily in our world as women *and* men become victims of someone else's lust. Lust is the opposite of love.

> Lust is selfish — Love is selfless
> Lust is wrong — Love is right
> Lust leaves you empty — Love leaves you satisfied
> Lust is hasty — Love is well planned
> Lust never lasts — Love never fails

The Bible gives a fairly graphic depiction of lust in action in the book of Proverbs. A young, foolish man is found being pursued by a seductive woman:

She took hold of him and kissed him
    and with a brazen face she said:
"Today I fulfilled my vows,
    and I have food from my fellowship offering at home.
So I came out to meet you;
    I looked for you and have found you!
I have covered my bed
    with colored linens from Egypt.
I have perfumed my bed
    with myrrh, aloes and cinnamon.
Come, let's drink deeply of love till morning;
    let's enjoy ourselves with love!
My husband is not at home;
    he has gone on a long journey.
He took his purse filled with money
    and will not be home till full moon."
With persuasive words she led him astray;
    she seduced him with her smooth talk.
All at once he followed her
    like an ox going to the slaughter,
like a deer stepping into a noose
    till an arrow pierces his liver,
like a bird darting into a snare,
    little knowing it will cost him his life. (Proverbs 7:13–23)

Although the words are from an ancient time, their meaning is as contemporary and common as those that surround us from all sides in the twenty-first century. Casual sex, one-night stands, sex buddies, "sexting" are all prevalent in our world. Those who are involved in sex outside of marriage are in the same danger as *"an ox going to the slaughter."* The consequences of sexual sins include guilt, fear of rejection, shame, sexually transmitted diseases and unwanted pregnancies.

When we read Paul's exhortation to Christians to *"flee from sexual immorality"* (1 Corinthians 6:18) and to avoid *"even a hint of sexual immorality, or...any kind of impurity"* (Ephesians 5:3) we are left with no doubt that our relationships with the opposite sex (as well as with the same sex) must be pure and innocent. Paul also instructed his young protégé Timothy to *"treat...younger women as sisters, with absolute purity"* (1 Timothy 5:2). Christians are commanded not to indulge in sexual immorality, and furthermore, to steer clear of any situation that might lead to an improper sexual relationship.

> *Can a man scoop fire into his lap*
> > *without his clothes being burned?*
> *Can a man walk on hot coals*
> > *without his feet being scorched?* (Proverbs 6:27–28)

Now that it's clear that sex is not meant to take place outside of marriage, what do we do to ensure that sexual love within marriage is fulfilling and enjoyable, the way God planned? It starts with the way we behave *before* marriage!

"Dating" is a relatively modern phenomenon that allows two people to interact and enjoy a friendly relationship. When we think of dating, we should not immediately assume we are looking for a marriage partner. In one sense, dating is a training ground to learn how to relate to the opposite sex properly. Going out with a small group of friends can be fun and relaxing; it doesn't need to be a stressful "test" to see if someone is "the one." That being said, unless you live in a culture of arranged marriages, dating is usually the process by which you will decide on a mate for life. How you treat your dating partner may very well reveal the kind of character that will exist in your marriage in the future. If you treat him or her with respect and purity, those qualities will more than likely persist in the marriage relationship. By placing value on one another's moral integrity before the wedding, you will be able to trust one another more after you say, "I do!" Purity is a demonstration that doing God's will is the highest and greatest desire in your hearts.

God has placed a "time tag" on sex. A time tag is a specific time that God has ordained when something can be allowed. For example, there is a time tag on the legal driving age. We don't want five-year-olds to be behind the wheel; children must wait until they are the proper age to drive a car. There is a time tag on when a person can buy alcohol. You could even say there are time tags on Christmas presents! ("Do not open 'till Christmas"!) Time tags are to be respected, and they build our character. By waiting until the honeymoon to have sex, a bride and groom have shown that they appreciate and revere God's time tag.

An important message needs to be given at this juncture for those who enter marriage without the benefit of a chaste past. Although that's not ideal, God has an answer for that as well. You might need to go back to "Love Secret 2: Forgiving Love" to be reminded of God's mercy for each of us. Nothing is outside of God's grace and forgiveness. When Paul listed some horrendous sexual sins in 1 Corinthians 6, he concluded with this statement: *"And that is what some of you were. But you were washed, you were sanctified, you were justified in the name of the Lord Jesus Christ and by the Spirit of our God"* (verse 11). Even with less than perfect sexual pasts, God transforms and heals sinners so that they can, at the right time, enjoy sexual love.

KAY: This point is personal. Although I was raised to be a "good girl," my convictions became watered down during my teen years. I entered into sexual relationships that were not God's plan for me. I'm grateful that God guided me to his word and that I could be forgiven for my sins of immorality. God changed me dramatically, and my baptism made me a "new creation" (2 Corinthians 5:17). Later, when I revealed the truth of my past to Randy, he wrestled with his feelings of disappointment. Although I knew he loved me dearly, he had hoped to marry a virgin! I could never change the physical aspects of my sins, but we both knew that God had transformed my heart and my very being. The following lines are from a poem that he wrote for me:

I've dreamed of love ideally;
I've dreamed of love divine.
I've dreamed of one pure woman;
I wanted one—all mine.

And my dream has not been broken,
For I've a virgin from above.
By God I'll have this dream come true
From one new birth of love.

This is also a good opportunity, though, to encourage those readers who are young. Making the decision to follow Jesus early in life will help you to steer clear of things that will be harder to overcome later. If you become a Christian when you are young, you are not only saved from the sins you have committed, but you are also saved from the sins (and consequences of the sins) you might have committed in the future if you hadn't been a Christian. You are saved from the pain, the scars and the potentially terrible memories that sexual sins leave behind. Never believe the lie that sex will bring you acceptance, popularity or love. Hold on to your convictions; you'll be glad you did.

Maximum Sex

We can't possibly have a chapter on sexual love without referring to the Bible's Song of Solomon. This beautiful poem is the story of two lovers, the king and his bride, who unashamedly express their passion for one another. In one of the most poignant verses, the bride recites these words:

Place me like a seal over your heart,
  like a seal on your arm;
for love is as strong as death,
  its jealousy unyielding as the grave.
It burns like blazing fire,
  like a mighty flame.
Many waters cannot quench love;
  rivers cannot sweep it away. (Song of Songs 8:6–7a)

The seal that the bride describes is the *chotham*, from a root meaning "to impress." A seal was the impression on official documents, letters or contracts. In the ancient world, a seal was vitally important. It was either worn on the finger as a signet ring or was carried on a string close to the breast, near the heart. A seal was used to authenticate a signature or to mark approval, indicating that something was real, genuine and authorized. A seal also carried the idea of protection: you couldn't tamper with something that had a seal. By comparing her love to the seal, the bride is saying that she wants to be firmly in his love, to always be remembered and to be constantly under his protection and care.

God's plan for sexual love bears a resemblance to "sealing" a man and woman to one another. Males and females are created in a manner that draws them to one another, but in different ways. Neuroscientists claim that a female releases oxytocin during sexual stimulation. This causes her to bond or be attached at a hormonal level, and eventually it becomes a conditioned response: oxytocin is released by seeing her lover. Males, on the other hand, have a different wiring. The impression that occurs during the first sexual experience(s) is not connected to the person as much as it is to the experience(s) itself. If the context is a lustful one, then he is headed down the road of seeing the sexual act as one that's only about himself and his pleasure. If the context is married love, then he is paving the way for a lifetime of love as he becomes emotionally "sealed" to the woman he adores. There's a lot more to it than that, obviously, but the simple fact is that God created sexual love to be a total-person experience. It is the cement that holds two people together. As Psalm 139:14 states, we are *"fearfully and wonderfully made."* In the New Living Translation this verse says, *"Thank you for making me so wonderfully complex! Your workmanship is marvelous."*

RANDY: *I have always been proud of Kay's and my dating relationship as disciples. We dated for over two years and let me tell you, I was infatuated, and drunk on love! Yeah, we were certainly the two in a crowd who only had eyes for each other. And we loved being together whenever we could. But I was never alone in her apartment with her, and she was never alone in my dorm room with me. That would be foolish. It would be like the guy and girl who sat alone on a bed and said to each other, "Let's pray we don't fall into temptation!" Our dates were almost always double dates, and I always got her home before midnight. I took the advice I'd heard to not touch a girl's body from the shoulders down and the knees up. We loved to hold hands and I loved to kiss her goodnight. We had a blast. Now don't get me wrong; there were certainly times of temptation, but we kept it pure. And on our wedding night, we had an unforgettable first sexual time together. I remember everything about it! For our wedding I had written a song that I entitled "Set Me as a Seal." Kay sang it to me in front of our families and a fairly large audience before we took our vows. She did an amazing job. I am forever "sealed" to my Kay! I will share the words with you.*

SET ME AS A SEAL
Randy McKean, 1976

Set me as a seal upon your heart,
A seal unbroken,
Never torn or apart.
Set me as a seal upon your arm,
A seal of honor
Never forgotten or harmed.

Today is our day,
A day in which by love we're adorned.
Today is our day,
A day of beauty like the world's first morn.
Today is our day,
For into God's loving grace we were born.

For near to you is where I want to be
For now, forever,
Always making my love free.
And from this day we'll never be apart;
I'm one with you
In soul, mind, body and heart.

Today is our day,
A day in which by love we're adorned.
Today is our day,
A day of beauty like the world's first morn.
Today is our day,
For into God's loving grace we were born.

Many waters cannot quench our love,
Nor can it be drowned by floods
From up above—
We had waited so very long for
Love to start—
So now set me as a seal
Upon your heart.

Today is our day,
A day in which by love we're adorned.
Today is our day,
A day of beauty like the world's first morn.
Today is our day,
For into God's loving grace we were born.

When you understand the value of God's way of sexual love, you will never want to trade it in for something of less value. Let's say you are shown two paintings, and you are deciding which one you like better. Maybe they look like they are worth about the same, but then you are told the value of each. One has a $50 value, and the other has a value of over one million dollars! Well, now which one are you drawn to? Which one do you want to have? The answer is obvious. Similarly, there is the cheap, easy, no commitment superficial sex that may look good at first but ends with many broken hearts, broken lives and broken dreams. It seems to satisfy, but when you put it up against the extraordinary value of sexual love that offers genuine and authentic love for a lifetime, there is no comparison. God's plan for sexual love allows for what we call maximum sex! Maximum sex leaves behind no guilt, shame or unwanted consequences because we live this wonderful part of our lives as we were created to live it. It brings about fulfillment, satisfaction and joy. This is a love between two people like no other. Marital love is the strongest, most steadfast and invincible force in the human experience.

> **1 Man (Married to) 1 Woman + Bible Defined Love = Maximum Sex**

Additionally, there is a simple secret to maximum sex. It's simple, but it doesn't mean it's easy. Within a marriage relationship, maximum sex occurs when a man and a woman can become so safe and so secure with one another that they can give freely of themselves to their partner. It involves a trust that can only occur with a couple who is committed to one another totally. This is what's described in 1 Corinthians 7:4: *"The wife does not have authority over her own body but yields it to her husband. In the same way, the husband does not have authority over his own body but yields it to his wife."* Portrayed in this way, sex is not a "getting" thing but a "giving" thing. And so there will be the meeting of each other's needs and wants sexually. This is encouraged by the understanding that it is just as wrong to say yes to the wrong person as it is to say no to the right person. Of course there is to be a selfless sensitivity to each other's health issues, emotional needs and physical tiredness. Furthermore, this scripture is saying to a spouse, in essence: "You, and only you, are the one I want to share my life, my heart and my body with. I give it to you totally, uniquely and wholeheartedly. You alone are the one who will cherish my body.

I belong to you." When both partners have these attitudes, both will be able to fully enjoy the pleasure of sexual love. And since God created us, including our sexual nature and its desires, he knows what breaks us and what bonds us. God did not make any mistakes!

Here are a few concluding thoughts from a *USA Today* article:

AHA! CALL IT THE REVENGE OF THE CHURCH LADIES
William R. Mattox

Sigmund Freud said they suffered from an "obsessional neurosis" accompanied by guilt, suppressed emotions and repressed sexuality. Former Saturday Night Live comedian, Dana Carvey, satirized them as uptight prudes who believe sex is downright dirty. But several major research studies show that church ladies (and the men who sleep with them) are among the most satisfied people on the face of the earth.... At least four factors appear to be responsible for the link between spiritual commitment and sexual fulfilment.

First, church ladies appear to benefit from their lack of sexual experience prior to marriage....

Second, churchgoers appear to benefit from a commitment to marital fidelity and marital permanence....

Third, church ladies typically enjoy far greater sexual freedom....The absence of sexual anxiety [makes them] free from guilt associated with violating one's own sexual standards....

Finally, church ladies appear to benefit from the belief that God created sex....

Put in another way, churchgoers are apt to delight in the Edenesque pleasure of "being naked and not ashamed" and of celebrating the "transcendent intimacy" found only in the marriage bed.

Interestingly, the Bible encourages such exultation. Not only does it contain an entire book (The Song of Songs) that celebrates marital intimacy, but it also contains other passages that say things like, *"Rejoice in the wife of your youth....Let her breasts satisfy you at all times; Be exhilarated always by her love"* (Proverbs 5:18–19).

Now, these religious teachings are apt to come as a shock to those who believe God is a cosmic killjoy when it comes to sexuality. But if one wants to know why church ladies are having so much fun, my best guess is that their husbands are actually taking these biblical passages quite literally.

And so Love Secret 9 concerning sexual love has three bold headlines:

Sex Is Good but It's Not Everything
Sex Is Good but It's Not Essential
Sex Is Good but It's Not for Everyone

LOVE SECRET 10

Discipling Love

Scroll down in your online dictionary, starting with the letters d-i-s-c-i-p-l. What will you find? Disciple, disciples, discipleship, disciplinarian, discipline, discipliner, disclaim...wait, did we miss the word "discipling"? Yes, we admit that the word can't be found. But the concept of discipling is found throughout the Scriptures, and discipling love is Love Secret 10. Discipling is all about loving people in the way Jesus loved people. As we commit ourselves to being his disciples (defined as one who learns, accepts, adheres to and advances the teaching of the one being followed) we are called to be in relationships with other disciples. These relationships we call discipling relationships.

"A new command I give you: Love one another. As I have loved you, so you must love one another. By this everyone will know that you are my disciples, if you love one another." (John 13:34–35)

Walk in the way of love, just as Christ loved us and gave himself up for us as a fragrant offering and sacrifice to God. (Ephesians 5:2)

Christian relationships can be the best, closest and most intimate relationships in this world. When you were a kid, did you ever vow to be "blood brothers" or "blood sisters" with a good friend? Perhaps you improvised on a ritual you had seen in old Western films: you made a pin prick in your finger to draw blood, and then pressed your finger to your friend's pricked finger. You "shared" blood, which made you as close as physical family—at least that was the idea. A Christian doesn't have to shed any blood to be related to other Christians. Jesus has already done that! We are brothers and sisters with those who share in the blood of Jesus. We are family! Within that family, having discipling relationships keeps us connected and more involved. To develop those relationships isn't complicated, but it does require effort and organization. Even physical families require organization to function well. And the bigger a family is, the more organization is needed. A family with twelve children requires more than a family with two children. Since most church congregations are usually large spiritual families, there is a need for lots of good organizing to keep the spiritual family close and functioning.

Why have discipling relationships? Obviously, we are all influenced by those we spend the most time with and those we feel connected to. We need to make sure those who influence us are going in the same direction we are going—the direction of following Jesus. Although we all come from different backgrounds, we have in common our commitment to Jesus as Lord. It's a beautiful thing to witness people from different nationalities, races, colors and languages enjoying fellowship with one another.

RANDY: The Northern Virginia Church of Christ, where I presently serve as an elder and an evangelist, is a glorious example of this. Our congregation consists of over 450 members. We are blessed to have among our members people from over fifty countries. Every year we celebrate what we call our International Day—a worship service designed to include and highlight the diversity of the church. It's so inspiring to hear songs sung and Jesus proclaimed as Lord in different languages. Many people wear the typical clothing of their countries, and everyone joins together for a meal, which is made complete by desserts from various international cuisines. This time together is a remarkable testimony to the command from Jesus to show that we are disciples by our love.

The differences we find in each other don't stop with just race or nationality. Added to this are the many types of personalities and the plethora of opinions that everyone brings into the family of Christ. Some people are better at navigating through these differences, and others must be trained (discipled) to love those who are very different from themselves. There will be times even in the best of relationships when someone sins against another. After all, even repentant and redeemed sinners are still sinners! So we continually learn how to remain united and remain loving. This is why we need discipling love.

One-Another Religion

Paul's letter to the church in Rome contains rich directives for loving one another. The Christians are urged to be devoted to God because of his wonderful grace and love (Romans 12:1–2). That devotion to God will show itself in devotion to others: *"For just as each of us has one body with many members, and these members do not all have the same function, so in Christ we, though many, form one body, and each member belongs to all the others"* (Romans 12:4–5). These are very important verses to comprehend. There are many members to both a physical body and a spiritual body (the church). They don't all provide the same functions for the body, but all are needed and necessary. Furthermore, every part of the body belongs to the body. In Christ's church, everyone "belongs"! No one can say, "Leave me alone" or "Stay out of my life." Paul's instructions go on to explain how everyone's strengths and gifts are there in order to serve and help each other. The involvement with one another is not a theoretical idea; every unique person has a role to fulfill within the body of Christ. Discipling relationships help us to put this passage into practice in our everyday lives.

"Love must be sincere" (Romans 12:9). Sincerity means purity, without deception or false pretense. There's an old story claiming that the word "sincere" originally meant "without wax." In an ancient marketplace, a buyer might be interested in a marble vase. He would ask the seller, "Is this sincere—without wax?" In other words, he was asking if the vase had cracks in it that had been filled and polished with wax. Although it looked perfect, he wanted to make sure it had no hidden flaws. While the origin of the story can be questioned, the illustration is a good one. Sincere love is honest and genuine, not just something that looks good on the outside. It is the real deal!

The passage in Romans 12 continues with specific ways regarding how Christians are to show love to each other. It includes being devoted to one another in love, honoring one another above ourselves and living in harmony with one another (verses 10, 16). These are just three of the many "one-another" passages that are found in the Bible. They are not one-another suggestions but one-another commands!

They define the ways that we can love like Jesus loved. Listed below are some of the one-another scriptures.

- Teach and counsel one another: Colossians 1:28–29
- Instruct one another: Romans 15:14
- Carry each other's burdens: Galatians 6:2
- Pray for each other: James 5:16
- Live in peace with each other: 1 Thessalonians 5:13
- Do what is good for each other: 1 Thessalonians 5:15
- Encourage one another daily: Hebrews 3:13
- Spur one another on toward love and good deeds: Hebrews 10:24
- Be kind and compassionate to one another: Ephesians 4:32
- Forgive each other: Ephesians 4:32
- Submit to one another: Ephesians 5:21
- Accept one another: Romans 15:7
- Confess your sins to one another: James 5:16

All of these one-another scriptures are perfectly summed up in Philippians 2:5: *"In your relationships with one another, have the same mindset as Christ Jesus."* We can't pick and choose the ones we like, but we must always be embracing and growing in all these ways of showing love. This is the way to love like Jesus.

Definition of Discipling Love

Our tenth love secret is Discipling Love. Discipling love is the implementation of the one-another religion that is commanded in the Bible and demonstrated in the life of Jesus. Discipling is a way to live out loving relationships that help both you and others to be all that God wants us to be. Discipling love is one of God's ways for us to mature in Christ. Without it, we cannot grow as God intended us to. These kinds of Christian relationships are not optional, although the implementation of discipling has plenty of flexibility. A good working definition of a discipling relationship is one in which friends are learning and practicing their Christianity together while having on-going, open conversations about their lives. They are guided by the expectation that God is their priority and that his word is the standard for their lives. Ultimately, they are training and helping each other make progress in becoming more like Jesus.

But before we go on, we need to put first things first. Our number one "discipler" (another made-up word, but it works!) is God. As we go through life—both the ups and the downs—before we look to anyone else for help we must first go to God in prayer and go to his word for wisdom, guidance and comfort. If you lack something, go to God first. If you need to change something, go to God first. If you need strength or wisdom or support, go to God first. But then, God's plan for living a Jesus life includes the right kind of loving involvement from other disciples. Everyone needs help from others to become a Christian and everyone needs help from others to live as a Christian. This is made clear in the Great Commission:

> *Then Jesus came to them and said, "All authority in heaven and on earth has been given to me. Therefore go and make disciples of all nations, baptizing them in the name of the Father and of the Son and of the Holy Spirit, and teaching them to obey everything I have commanded you. And surely I am with you always, to the very end of the age."* (Matthew 28:18–20)

Jesus commissioned his disciples to go and make other disciples—to help others to become Christians. But it doesn't end there. After baptism, Christians are to be taught to obey everything that Jesus taught the first disciples. Obedience is a lifetime challenge, and we need all the help we can get. We need to be taught how to live as a disciple. We need help to mature as a disciple. We need help to become an effective and fruitful disciple. We need teaching, guidance, encouragement, direction, correction and at times, although not very often, a rebuke to stay the course and obey the commandments. This is love. This is discipling love. It helps us get all the way to heaven!

Those of us who chose to become disciples of Jesus chose to obey him. Discipling love is what will help us do the very thing we want to do and desire to do. Discipling relationships don't make us obey, they help us to obey. Isn't it great to know that grace continues to forgive us? People have been baptized and all their sins are forgiven, but they are not perfect. They need to continue to be perfected. Being able to change and make progress in our Christian life is awesome. And God's plan is for every Christian to have the biblical relationships that will help them to become more and more like Jesus.

Discipling love is all about Jesus. Let's look at Colossians 1:28–29:

[Jesus] is the one we proclaim, admonishing and teaching everyone with all wisdom, so that we may present everyone fully mature in Christ. To this end I strenuously contend with all the energy Christ so powerfully works in me.

It's Jesus that we proclaim! It's Jesus' standard we live by. It's Jesus' life we model. JESUS...JESUS...JESUS! We are not just members of some religious social club. We are serious about living to become more like Jesus. So Love Secret 10 concerning discipling love is:

Discipling Love Is All About Jesus

It still starts with God—your ultimate discipler, trainer, teacher, coach and mentor. Relationships with humans are not most important. They can never be a replacement for God. But, as we have already said, people are a part of God's plan.

"And the things you have heard me say in the presence of many witnesses entrust to reliable people who will also be qualified to teach others" (2 Timothy 2:2). Entrust is a financial term. It means "to set something aside that is valuable." Here, Paul charges Timothy to deposit the Christian life that has been demonstrated and taught to him into other men. The progression would look like this:

Paul → Timothy → Faithful Men → who teach others

It's a multiplying effect to help mature the most people possible. A continual emphasis on raising up leaders through discipling love is a must for a church to have sustained growth and vitality. In fact, this passage was written to reproduce leaders like Paul, Timothy and the apostles, but because we all are to lead on some level, we can apply it to everyone. Husbands lead their wives. Parents lead their children. All are to lead individuals to Christ. All are to lead individuals to become more mature in Christ. So, this concept is right for the maturing and multiplication of the entire church. Jesus is the one who originally set the example of Christian discipling for us to follow. Jesus had different layers of relationships as we all do. Those layers would look something like this:

Jesus→John→Peter, James, John→the 12→
the 72→the 500→the multitudes

Jesus' closest relationship on earth seemed to be with his disciple John. Along with John, Peter and James shared an intimacy at special times and places, such as on the Mount of Transfiguration or in the Garden of Gethsemane. Expanding the circle, the twelve apostles traveled together, witnessed miracles together and learned together. Jesus concentrated most of his time with these few so his ministry could multiply to help the many. His ministry included the seventy-two that he sent out ahead of him, and he showed himself to the 500 after his resurrection. He taught multitudes at different times. But his focus was primarily on the few. These few matured and became effective and fruitful leaders for the first-century church. That was his plan then, and it must be imitated in our plan today!

We all need true friends in this life. We can still hear our moms say to us, "To make a friend, you have to be a friend." In a recent interview about the culmination of a seventy-five-year Harvard research project, the longest study on happiness in history, it was found that relationships are the key to a happy life. The headline actually said that this is what the Harvard project *discovered.* We would say Jesus knew about it a long time before Harvard did. In this study, people's lives were tracked through the years. The happiest and healthiest participants were the ones who maintained close, intimate relationships. It reported that wealth, fame and career success will not ultimately bring people health or happiness. It's the work they put into maintaining connections with other human beings that will. Here are a few quotes from the Washington Post article:

- People who are more isolated than they want to be from others find that they are less happy, their health declines earlier in midlife, their brain functioning declines sooner and they live shorter lives than people who are not lonely.

- Relationships are messy and they're complicated, and the hard work of tending to family and friends—it's not sexy or glamorous. It's also lifelong. It never ends.
- Quality and intimacy, as well as stability and consistency also matter. Casual relationships, like the ones on social media won't do; neither will contentious ones like an abusive marriage or an unreliable friend.

So the right kind of friends are vital for life (did we really need a Harvard report to tell us this?) and they take a lot of effort to have and maintain. We like the saying that tells us about the three kinds of friends: friends for a reason, friends for a season and friends for a lifetime. In the world of discipling love, the friendships that are forged will fit into these different categories as we travel through life. Not everyone is going to be a friend for life, but God has different people in our lives at different times for different reasons. Ultimately, they are to help us become more like Jesus.

Getting back to Jesus and Paul, they were not married and they had no children. So, if you are a married man or woman with children, your discipling methods won't look exactly the same as theirs—living together and traveling everywhere together, and so forth. But we can take the concept and live it out while embracing our life situations and our life circumstances. Jesus had fun, life-changing memories that he built with his friends. And isn't that how you make friends? It's the memories you build together. A lot of good memories produce a lot of good feelings. Jesus and his friends hiked together. They fished together. They went sailing together. They ate together. They even went water skiing together *without* the skis!

In order to grow in our love and in our imitation of Jesus, there are two convictions that we need to embrace:

1. I need discipling relationships!
2. Everyone needs discipling relationships!

After all, our life's circumstances keep changing. Careers go through different phases and challenges. Marriages go through different phases and challenges. Families go through different phases and challenges. With the aging process, we go through different phases and challenges. We are always moving into a new life situation or a new life season. It is humbling to admit to ourselves that we need help and encouragement, but humility is a good thing! The basic attitude we need to maintain is, "I've never been here before in my life, so I need to learn from those who have lived it successfully." Also, "I can learn from people who openly share their sins and mistakes so I don't have to fall into the same pits."

Good marriage discipling. Good family discipling. Good individual discipling. All are needed. It would be nice if it just happened, but it doesn't. That's why we need some organization to encourage it and help it to happen. We live in a busy society and culture, so it takes planning and commitment to have a good discipling relationship. You might be able to have a few "experts" in the church helping you from time to time with your marriage, parenting, finances or some other need, but what's needed on a regular basis is people who know you personally. Having a set time and a kept time to meet with a person or group that is committed to each other for discipling makes it work in our busy lives. Each person is to concentrate on a few at a time; the body is to minister to itself. Leaders and ministry staff can't meet the needs of all the people in a church. They are called by God to equip the members for works of service, not to do the works of service for the members. Each member of a church does their share of the work by speaking the truth in love and helping one another become more like Christ. All of these directives are found in Ephesians 4:11–16:

> *So Christ himself gave the apostles, the prophets, the evangelists, the pastors and teachers, to equip his people for works of service, so that the body of Christ may be built up until we all reach unity in the faith and in the knowledge of the Son of God and become mature, attaining to the whole measure of the fullness of Christ.*
>
> *Then we will no longer be infants, tossed back and forth by the waves, and blown here and there by every wind of teaching and by the cunning and craftiness of people in their deceitful scheming. Instead, speaking the truth*

in love, we will grow to become in every respect the mature body of him who is the head, that is, Christ. From him the whole body, joined and held together by every supporting ligament, grows and builds itself up in love, as each part does its work.

The discipling love concept is biblical. It's the way people in the church are to relate to one another. The method of application and the name you give this application are a matter of opinion, but the principle of having other people involved in your life to help you spiritually is a matter of obedience.

Discipling Truths

- Discipling reinforces the concept of the body ministering to itself as people use their gifts and talents to love others. Those who are better at something can help others to make progress in their Christian life (marriage, family, purity, Bible knowledge, helping the poor and needy, prayer, etc.).

- Discipling translates biblical truth into practical living by applying the Bible to life situations as they arise.

- Discipling develops character qualities in the lives of Christians. Character development involves doing, and discipling is all about doing things together.

- Discipling is not limited to a classroom or to a set time. It can occur any time, any place. As we are told in Deuteronomy 6:6–7 concerning the discipling of children: *"These commandments that I give you today are to be on your hearts. Impress them on your children. Talk about them when you sit at home and when you walk along the road, when you lie down and when you get up."*

- Discipling is not overly structured. It's a way of life and a way of thinking.

- Discipling is not a program; it's done in the context of relationships, not written lessons.

How Do We Learn?

The Greek word for disciple is *mathetes,* which means one who learns and takes instruction. We are to be learners all our lives. God places us in the church in order that we can learn from one another. How do we learn? An old Chinese Proverb contains a lot of truth:

> I hear, and I forget.
> I see, and I remember.
> I do, and I understand.

Psychologists say we have a potential of remembering 10% of what we hear. If we add seeing to hearing the potential for remembering goes up to 50%. If we add doing to hearing and seeing it brings it up to 90%. Discipling is the 90% kind of learning! It's walking with someone for a period of time. God created the learning process to be like this, and so God uses it for our spiritual development. It is God's way for us to grow, to mature, to learn, to develop. The apostle Paul put it in these words:

> *Whatever you have learned or received or heard from me, or seen in me—put it into practice. And the God of peace will be with you. (Philippians 4:9)*

> *Follow my example, as I follow the example of Christ. (1 Corinthians 11:1)*

A Little of God's Wisdom

Proverbs 15:22–23

> *Plans fail for lack of counsel,*
> *but with many advisers they succeed.*
> *A person finds joy in giving an apt reply—*
> *and how good is a timely word!*

Help and input from those who have succeeded is what leads us to have success in all aspects of life. And both receiving and giving timely words brings joy to our lives.

Proverbs 18:17

> *In a lawsuit the first to speak seems right,*
> *until someone comes forward and cross-examines.*

We see things from our own point of view and so we present our own cases all the time. We all need input from others to gain a more objective understanding of ourselves.

Proverbs 20:18

> *Plans are established by seeking advice;*
> *so if you wage war, obtain guidance.*

Everyone needs guidance. Wise instruction gives us victory in many of life's situations.

Proverbs 27:17

> *As iron sharpens iron,*
> *so one person sharpens another.*

How is our inner person sharpened? One important way is through another individual. If all you want to know is how you look on the outside, then any mirror will do. The best mirror to your inner self is a close friend.

What Discipling Love Is NOT

In any fellowship, different people have had different experiences with relationships. Whether it's relationships with parents, siblings, a spouse or with children, most everyone has had some good and some bad experiences. But it would be a wrong reaction if a person who has had a bad experience were to throw out the concept of family, marriage or childbearing. In the same way, people have had different experiences in the church with discipling relationships, some good and, possibly, some bad. It would be a wrong reaction to throw out the concept of discipling relationships based on some bad experiences! However, it's helpful to know what discipling is by knowing what it's not.

1. Discipling Love is NOT...the only way to mature in Christ. There are additional ways that God will provide in order to help us grow. But discipling love is prescribed as a way to biblically bring people to maturity in Christ, which is what God wants for all of his children.

2. Discipling Love is NOT...being fully responsible to get another person to heaven. Each person is individually responsible for their own spiritual salvation (Philippians 2:12–13). We should not be over-responsible for others.

3. Discipling Love is NOT...having authority over another person's life. The word of God is the ultimate authority and it is what must be used in a discipling relationship. Some words spoken often to each other should be "Let's look and see what the Bible has to say" and "What do you think Jesus would do?" God's will is absolute and clear in many, many things. At times, we must wrestle to seek God's will for our lives (Romans 12:1–2). There may not be a specific command (Do I move to Miami?) but there will be biblical principles to apply. In many decisions, there is more than one option that would be in the will of God. Also, keep in mind that many things are matters of opinion but as disciples we want to strive to do what is best, not just what is OK. And so, there are times we need help and input from others in wrestling through to God's will.

4. Discipling Love is NOT...primarily confession of sin. It should be primarily encouragement. Certainly we will all need help to deal with our sin from time to time. Discipling times would not be something to look forward to if confession of sin was the expectation every time or even most times we met together. When a person is wrestling with a particular sin, they carry the responsibility

to confess it and get the help they need. Discipling love is not about being a sin detective.

5. Discipling Love is NOT...primarily confronting what needs to change in a person. It is to be an ongoing conversation about life between two friends helping each other become more like Christ. It is walking together. It is seeing a positive example of Christianity so we can better know how to live it effectively. With one another we are to help, urge, be patient, be full of encouragement, be full of teaching from God's word and be full of prayer. There will be times when we need to confront and point out specific things but this is done lovingly and gently.

6. Discipling Love is NOT...meeting all a person's needs. Individuals are to meet their own personal needs primarily (Galatians 6:1–5). There are times we need to bear one another's burdens when a person's life's load is just too heavy to carry alone. But no person can or should try to meet all of another person's needs. Relying on just one person to provide everything is unhealthy. That's why we have the body of Christ; different people will be able to help in different ways. Even those who are married should learn this lesson. Husbands and wives need other friendships and should not place the burden for meeting every need on their spouse.

7. Discipling Love is NOT...an accountability time. It is a time to talk, share and gain direction, spiritual perspective and spiritual input. It can be a time to "do" Christianity together, for example praying together, reaching out to others, or serving the poor together. There may be times when one might ask to be held accountable on a particular area of their life, but this won't define the relationship. As a matter of fact, the world understands the need for accountability—think of physical fitness trainers as well as diet groups, Alcoholics Anonymous and other groups. While discipling relationships will include accountability, it should not be the main focus of the times together.

What Discipling Love IS

Discipling love is the help we need to make progress in becoming like Jesus. Our goal and desire is to become like our perfect savior. That's a very high call, and it might seem overwhelming at times! But what God is looking for is progress. As we make progress we can be happy with ourselves and others can be happy with us.

RANDY: I am so thankful for the countless number of people through the years who have made an impact through discipling love to help me make progress in becoming more like Jesus. Many people have given me joy, help, encouragement, fun, refreshment, teaching, friendship, spiritual connection and godly challenge. I have been helped to a great degree in my marriage, my family, my ministry and my individual walk with God. I also enjoy (most of the time!) the discipling love I receive from my wife. In fact, one of our greatest discipling resources through the years has been each other. And what a joy it has been for us to raise our children with discipling love. Our family devotionals together and individual parent/ child times have allowed us to develop great relationships. We don't have a perfect marriage or a perfect family, but we are still making progress as we are all becoming more like Christ. My discipling relationships with my son and my daughter as they were growing up are among my most cherished memories.

Discipling love is helping to form Jesus in each of us. Everything we do with each other is to be Jesus-centered. Every conversation is to help point us to Jesus. Every concern we have for each other is to be Jesus focused. Then we are to live like Jesus. We think we need all the help and encouragement we can get to do that, don't you? We also think God has a great plan to deliver that help and encouragement to us. We will close this chapter out with a poem that says it clearly—it's all about Jesus. And so, Love Secret 10 is...

Discipling Love Is All About Jesus

THE "WITH JESUS" LIFE

Steve Kinnard

(Inspired by the closing of a Ray Steadman sermon)

Jesus through the night.
Jesus at sunrise.
Jesus when the alarm rings.
Jesus with the first cup of coffee.
Jesus in our quiet time.
Jesus in our morning workout.
Jesus as we leave the house.
Jesus on the morning commute.
Jesus in the work place.
Jesus on the campus.
Jesus when we take a test.

Jesus at lunchtime.
Jesus during the afternoon slump.
Jesus on the commute home.
Jesus at the dinner table.
Jesus on a relaxing evening.

Jesus on the golf course.
Jesus on the football pitch.
Jesus playing X-Box.
Jesus at the movies.
Jesus at Starbucks.
Jesus at the mall.
Jesus in the living room.
Jesus when we're far from home.
Jesus when we are surfing the Net.
Jesus when we answer email.
Jesus in our text messages.
Jesus when we're on the phone.

Jesus when we serve the poor.
Jesus when we encourage a friend.
Jesus when we go to bed.
Jesus when we sleep.
Jesus when we dream.

Jesus when we wake up.
Jesus for each new day.
Jesus in every single thing we do.
Jesus in every word.
Jesus in every conversation.
Jesus in every joke.
Jesus in every comment.
Jesus when we sneeze.

Jesus in every moment.
Jesus in every space.
Jesus in every relationship.
Jesus with Mom and Dad.
Jesus with our spouse.
Jesus with our kids.
Jesus with our neighbors.

Jesus in every action.
Jesus in every inaction.
Jesus when we're alone.
Jesus with our enemies.
Jesus with our friends.

Jesus when we're up or down.
Jesus when we're gray or blue.
Jesus when we are on top of the world.
Jesus when the world's on top of us.

Jesus in good times. Jesus in bad.
Jesus in feast.
Jesus in famine.
Jesus in joy.
Jesus in sorrow.
Jesus in ecstasy.
Jesus in tragedy.
Jesus in pleasure.
Jesus in pain.
Jesus in strength.
Jesus in weakness.
Jesus in smiles.
Jesus in frowns.

Jesus up,
Jesus down,
Jesus right,
Jesus left,
Jesus forward,
Jesus behind,
and Jesus in between.
Jesus inside,
Jesus outside,
Jesus upside down.
Jesus three-sixty.
Jesus twenty-four/seven.

Jesus with us.
The "with Jesus" life.

Jesus, Jesus I love thee.
What a friend we have in Jesus.
'Tis so sweet to trust in Jesus.
Jesus is all the world to me.
Jesus loves me, this I know.
Jesus keep me near the cross.
Take the world but give me Jesus.
Jesus, lover of my soul.
Anywhere with Jesus I can safely go.
Safe in the arms of Jesus.
Stand up, stand up for Jesus.
I have decided to follow Jesus.
Clothed in Jesus.
Wrapped in Jesus.
Enveloped in Jesus.
Encircled in Jesus.
Enmeshed in Jesus.
Engulfed in Jesus.
And even embalmed in Jesus.

Maranatha.
Come, oh Lord.
Come quickly, King Jesus.

PART FOUR

RESPONSE TO LOVE

We have already seen that God is love and that Jesus reveals love to us in a flesh-and-blood kind of way. Furthermore, we have delved into 10 Love Secrets that have given insight, inspiration, direction and practical application for the love we are to have flowing out of our relationship with God. Now we want to look at the big picture to see our response to the love of God. What are we to do with this incredible gift of Jesus dying on the cross for us? The answer is quite simple. We are to love God back. But what is the right way to do this? What is the right frame of mind to do it in? How are we supposed to view our lives now that we know of God's love for us and want to return that love?

RANDY: I will never forget falling in love with Kay. I remember the first time I ever saw her. It was in a crowd at my first Christian conference...the 1974 Florida Evangelism Seminar. She was walking one way and I was walking the other way in a crowded hallway as we were going to different classes. Of course she didn't notice me but she caught my eye. And I remember the second time I ever saw her, a few weeks later. I was leading the communion service on a Sunday evening. She had blond hair, blue eyes and a great shape. Yep...I was attracted to her looks. The deeper attraction came when I really got to know her. She was full of life, had a happy personality, was fun loving and had a heart for God. She was serious about her commitment to Jesus. She had a changed life, from an agnostic, partying sorority girl to a lover of God. Our first date was on February 8, 1975. I was eighteen years old and a sophomore in college. Two months later we had our second date. It was what was called Play Day, which was an all-day church picnic. When I took her home and said goodbye I decided she was the one for me. I never dated anyone else. (She did, but that's another story for another time!)

I was in love. I remember well the excitement and the joy of each next date. I enjoyed getting to know who she was as a person—her likes and dislikes, how she viewed life, what she had experienced in life and what her dreams were for her life. I remember the first time I told her I loved her. That was a scary time. What if she was just silent? What if she just said, "Thanks"? What if she said, "I love you too...like a brother"? But she told me she loved me! WOW...my heart went to the moon! Being in love meant I wanted to make her happy. I wrote poems, gave her cards, took her on walks, had creative dates (translation: cheap dates!) and we prayed together. Just to hold hands was electric and special. We dated for two years. We kept our relationship totally pure and then we got married. I will never forget Kay coming down the aisle in her white dress. I was thinking to myself, "I can't believe she loves ME!" Now, that's our love story. I'll never forget it. It's now thirty-nine years since our wedding day and I'm still in love. I must always keep and protect this love.

But then there's my love story with God—an even more important love story. And just like my love story with Kay, I remember the growing feelings, the passion, the excitement, the joy, the desire to spend time together. I remember coming out of the waters of baptism as a new man and thinking, "I can't believe God loves ME!" It's been forty-three years since my baptism and I'm still in love. I must always keep and protect this love.

A picture is worth a thousand words...or so they say. Well, at least we all like pictures and illustrations. As children, we liked to look at the pictures in a book. It made the story come alive for us. As grade-school kids, we liked pictures because it meant we had to read less in our homework assignments! But as adults, maybe they help us to better remember what the words are trying to say. Maybe they make the point in such a way that we can grasp it and then retain it longer. So we will make the use of some simple illustrations in this chapter as we move through it.

FOUNDATION OF LIFE

1. Stand by Grace

What is the picture of our response to God? First we must have a strong foundation. There are three layers to this foundation. We call it the FOUNDATION OF LIFE. The first layer is grace. Everything else gets built on this. We are enabled to stand before God only by his grace. Salvation, forgiveness and our relationship with God are each an undeserved gift. We can't earn them or merit them or ever become good enough to deserve them. They are given to us by the mercy, love and goodness of God. Salvation is a free gift. Ephesians 2:4–5, 8–9 states it this way: *"But because of his great love for us, God, who is rich in mercy, made us alive with Christ even when we were dead in transgressions—it is by grace you have been saved....and this is not from yourselves, it is the gift of God—not by works, so that no one can boast."* What allows us to stand saved in this life is God's **R**iches **A**t **C**hrist's **E**xpense. We STAND BY GRACE.

STAND BY GRACE

2. Love God by Choice

The second layer of the foundation is our individual response to God's love. In any relationship, someone has to love first. God loved us first by sending his Son to die in our place (1 John 4:10). We are to respond to God with the decision to love him. After all, this is the first and the greatest commandment. All must understand that love has feelings attached to it but love is primarily a decision. Feelings go up and down; a decision remains constant regardless of the feelings of the moment.

RANDY & KAY: We got married thirty-nine years ago. Our feelings for each other were quite strong that day. During our marriage years, our feelings at times have become both stronger and weaker than on our wedding day. We have had our sad times, our disappointing times, our challenging times, our misunderstanding times, our sickly times and our selfish times within our marriage. During these periods, our feelings have gone up or down to some degree. But our decision to love each other has remained constant. And we are happy to report that there have been many more good and happy times than bad and sad times. (A lot more ups than downs!) We have been faithful to each other and we will continue to be faithful to each other, come what may. Why? Because we made the decision to love.

Our decision to love God must be a lifetime decision—for better or worse; for richer or poorer; in sickness and in health. And certainly our love for God extends into love for Jesus. He's the Son of God, God in the flesh, the one who loved us by volunteering for a substitutionary death. He accepted the death penalty for our sin so we could be set free. So, this second layer for the foundation of life is LOVE GOD BY CHOICE: *"Jesus replied: 'Love the Lord your God with all your heart and with all your soul and with all your mind. This is the first and greatest commandment'"* (Matthew 22:37–38).

LOVE GOD BY CHOICE

STAND BY GRACE

3. Live by Faith

The third layer of our Christian foundation is faith. A response of faith must be entwined with our response of love, because trust is in the very definition of love. According to the Hebrew writer, faith is being sure of what we hope for and certain of what we do not see. In fact we cannot please God without faith. Galatians 2:20b states: *"The life I now live in the body, I live by faith in the Son of God, who loved me and gave himself for me."* This clearly declares that in the new life with Christ, we are to live by faith. We find this phrase also in 2 Corinthians 5:7: *"For we live by faith, not by sight."* We recommend that you read the book *Radical Faith—10 Faith Secrets*. The 10 Faith Secrets will make faith in God work personally, powerfully and persistently for you! Biblically, saving faith has three distinct parts:

- We are to believe the facts.
- We are to trust the promises.
- We are to obey the commandments.

With this third layer, the foundation for life is completed. We are to LIVE BY FAITH.

PURPOSE OF LIFE

Now that we are standing on the Foundation of Life, we need to know what we are standing under—what the overarching purpose of our lives is. This covering is the PURPOSE OF LIFE. All that the Christian is about and does is to fall under or be enclosed by this covering. This covering gives insight into the meaning of life. Why are we here? What is life really all about? How was I created to live? What am I to be accomplishing with my life? How do I make my life count for the right things? What is worth living for? These are big questions that need direction and understanding for us to live fulfilled, satisfied and happy lives. This covering of the Purpose of Life has only one layer, but it is expressed in three very distinct ways.

1. All for the Glory of God

> *So whether you eat or drink or whatever you do, do it all for the glory of God.* (1 Corinthians 10:31)

We understand that the specific context of this passage is maintaining unity with matters of opinion, yet it states a universal truth as it covers everything we do. WHATEVER you do, do it all for the glory of God. That covers the totality of our lives! This is the purpose of our lives—all we do is for the glory of God.

What we do and what we don't do...is for the glory of God. What we say and what we don't say...is for the glory of God. Where we go and where we don't go...is for the glory of God. Who we associate with and who we don't associate with...is for the glory of God. How we act and how we don't act...is for the glory of God. How we react and how we don't react...is for the glory God. Our job or schoolwork or profession is for the glory of God. Our family is for the glory of God. Our marriage is for the glory of God. Any talent is for the glory of God. Our money is for the glory of God. Our time is for the glory of God. ALL is for the glory of God!

Paul includes himself when he writes in the first chapter of Ephesians that those who were first to put their hope in Christ might be (exist) for the praise of God's glory. Now, what does this word glory mean? It means to magnify, extol, praise and ascribe honor to God. It is to acknowledge God—his being, his attributes, his deeds. To glorify God is our highest purpose and noblest work. This is our fundamental reason for being. Giving glory to God continues into eternity.

Then I heard what sounded like a great multitude, like the roar of rushing waters and like loud peals of thunder, shouting:

"Hallelujah!
For our Lord God Almighty reigns.
Let us rejoice and be glad
and give him glory!" (Revelation 19:6-7a)

So our entire lives are to be under this covering: FOR THE GLORY OF GOD. If something does not glorify God then it should not be in our lives. We should ask ourselves as we go through the days of our lives, "Does this bring glory to God?"

2. Jesus is Lord

The second way The Purpose of Life can be expressed is in the phrase "Jesus is Lord." These are the words spoken and the promise made at our public confession of faith (in front of few or many people) before our baptism into Christ for the forgiveness of sins.

If you declare with your mouth, "Jesus is Lord," and believe in your heart that God raised him from the dead, you will be saved. (Romans 10:9)

Fight the good fight of the faith. Take hold of the eternal life to which you were called when you made your good confession in the presence of many witnesses. (1 Timothy 6:12)

With these words we are pledging to make Jesus our master, leader, commander, king, ruler, director, teacher, shaper, manager, overseer, head and authority in our lives. Jesus becomes our supreme example, and we promise to follow in his steps. Our purpose and goal in life is now to become more and more like him. Although made trite in our world today with T-shirts and wristbands, the poignant question that should be daily in our mind and heart is, "What would Jesus do?" *"Whoever claims to live in him must live as Jesus did"* (1 John 2:6).

3. Walk in Love

Follow God's example, therefore, as dearly loved children and walk in the way of love, just as Christ loved us and gave himself up for us as a fragrant offering and sacrifice to God. (Ephesians 5:1–2)

As you have heard from the beginning, his command is that you walk in love. (2 John 6b)

Follow the way of love. (1 Corinthians 14:1a)

Do everything in love. (1 Corinthians 16:14)

The third expression of The Purpose of Life is to walk in the way of love. The way of love is the very definition of who God is and what Jesus embodied and demonstrated for us when he lived as a man on this planet. And since love is an eternal entity as opposed to faith and hope, which will pass away (faith becomes sight and hope becomes reality), it is an overall covering and expression of purpose for our lives.

The word "walk" is referring to a person's behavior, conduct, habits or lifestyle. Therefore, actions of love are to define a person. According to God through the apostle Paul, love is the most excellent way. There is no better or greater way to live. The important factor is that it must be God's way of love and not the world's way of love. The two must not be confused. Sadly, men and women have distorted, redefined and corrupted true love, along with many other things. Once we understand God's way of love (the purpose of this book!), the day-to-day question we must pose to ourselves as we journey through life is, "What is the loving thing to do?"

ALL FOR THE GLORY OF GOD
JESUS IS LORD
WALK IN LOVE

LIVE BY FAITH

LOVE GOD BY CHOICE

STAND BY GRACE

SPECIFICS OF LIFE

The Foundation of Life holds us. The Purpose of Life defines us. And now we come to the Specifics of Life that direct us. There are eight specific directives that encompass the responsibilities of the Christian life.

We like the word "privileges" much better than "responsibilities" as we consider these eight Specifics of Life, because we do feel it to be a great privilege and an honor to love God in all of these ways. It's what we get to do instead of what we have to do. Beyond that, it is what we were created to do. Any relationship comes with responsibilities, but if a relationship is built on love, it's not considered a duty or a burden. Even though there are times when a married couple may not feel like carrying out the chores of a household, they do the right thing regardless of feelings. There is a desire to please the other person with the understanding that they don't have to be married, they get to be married. And in the same way, we don't have to live the Christian life; we get to live the Christian life!

The Specifics of Life are:

1. **Personal Life**—Personal Relationship with God/Personal Righteousness/Personal Needs – We must build and sustain our personal relationship with God through prayer, fasting and the study of God's word. We must be alert about our personal righteousness as we strive to become more and more like Jesus. We need to deal with the sins and temptations in our lives. And we must meet our own personal needs. This certainly includes taking care of ourselves physically and emotionally.

2. **Public Worship**—We are to gather together with other believers for public singing, teaching, preaching, communion, contribution and fellowship. This is not just an "add-on" but is essential for any Christian.

3. **Personal Relationships with Brothers and Sisters in Christ**—We are to be developing and maintaining relation-

ships that put into practice the one-another commands—serve one another, encourage one another, pray for one another, etc. This certainly would include having discipling relationships as was discussed in Love Secret 10.

4. **Profession or School**—We are to work as if we are working for the Lord. Without allowing our job or schoolwork to become a sinful priority, we are to excel as we do our very best at school and at work.

5. **The Poor and Needy**—We are to develop and maintain a heart that moves us to meet the physical needs of the poor, especially if they are our brothers and sisters in Christ.

6. **Proclaiming Jesus**—Our mission on this earth is to seek and save the lost. To accomplish this we must invite, befriend and study the Bible with people on an ongoing, lifestyle basis. We do this to teach them the gospel—the good news of Jesus. We encourage and persuade people to make the decision to believe, to repent, to make Jesus Lord and to be baptized for the forgiveness of sin.

7. **Parents and Children**—We are to honor, obey and respect our parents. This would certainly include taking care of them to the extent it is needed in their old age. If we have children, they are a blessing from God and a wonderful responsibility as we bring them up in the Lord. Fathers are given the specific charge to be the spiritual leader in the home—to bring the children up in the training and instruction of the Lord.

8. **Partner in Marriage**—If you have a husband or wife, then developing and maintaining a loving relationship becomes a great priority in the mind of God. Husbands are given the special charge to lead and love their wives as Christ does the church. Wives are given the special charge to respect and submit to their husbands.

All these *Specifics of Life* fall under the covering of the *Purpose of Life* as we stand on the *Foundation of Life*.

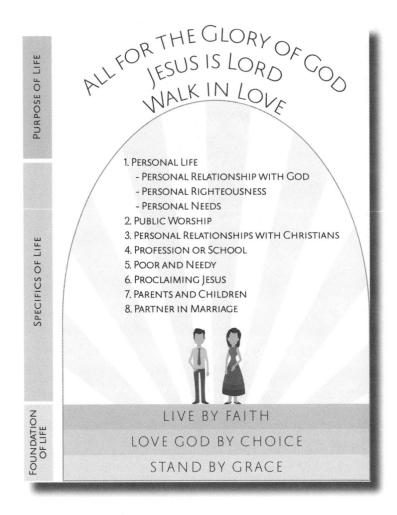

This should give us the picture of what our lives look like as disciples of Jesus. But before we completely finish it, let's put a few final touches on it and bring it into focus with Ultra-HD clarity. We are to give careful thought to our way of life. There are 10 biblical concepts we must grasp and apply if we are to live our response to God's love successfully and correctly.

Concept 1: It's All or Nothing!

All the Specifics of Life are to be consistently embraced and lived out, or our lives will not glorify God. If a student taking eight classes brought home a report card with six A's and two F's, the problem is obviously not intellectual ability. The problem is most likely that the student doesn't like two of the subjects or thinks of them as unimportant; therefore the student is not putting any effort into them. We would not consider this person a good student; there is a problem that first must be corrected. But if you have a student who has eight classes and brings home four A's, two B's, and two C's and has done the very best of their ability, then we would call this person a good student. In a similar way (although we understand that this is just an analogy and that God is not grading us in this manner), if we as a disciple or student of Jesus are doing well with six of the Specifics of Life and just ignoring two of them because they are more difficult or not as enjoyable or not important to us, we would not be a good student of Jesus. What God wants is for us to strive to do our very best in all the Specifics of Life. No one is best at everything. That's one good reason he put us in the church, his body, so that one person's weaknesses can be covered by another person's strengths. Then when someone looks at the body of Christ, they really do see Jesus. All the Specifics of Life are of the same importance and so all of them are to be a continual focus in our lives. So here's the bottom line: Our lives do not glorify God unless we are fully living and fully embracing ALL of the Christian life. This could also be said using the other statements of purpose. For instance, Jesus is either the Lord of all or he is not our Savior at all. Also, since a walk is made up of many steps, we are no longer walking in love if we refuse to obey all the steps of love. It's all or nothing.

Concept 2: It's Never OK to Say No to God

The Christian life is not pick-and-choose, as we have just seen. It's not a cafeteria line where we take what we want and refuse what we don't want. In the many years we have been Christians (Randy forty-three years, Kay forty-two years) and have been in the full-time ministry (thirty-six years), we have noted that one of the first Christian responsibilities people let go of is proclaiming Jesus. They let go of their evangelism. We think this is true because the tendency for people is to find it a difficult command to obey. It takes courage. It takes patience. It takes kindness. It takes perseverance. It takes time. In other words, it takes love.

Seeking and saving the lost is our mission in life. We certainly do this by letting our light shine as we allow people to see our marriages, our families, how we work at our job, and other areas of our lives. But we cannot do our mission successfully if we do not also open our mouths. Everyone has to invite people to church and Bible studies. Everyone has to share the Scriptures with people as we share our lives with them as well. Actually it would be quite arrogant for anyone to think their life alone was good enough to bring someone to Christ. Jesus was perfect here on earth while everyone else is far from perfect and yet he, the perfect one, found it necessary to open his mouth to effectively make disciples for God.

Going along with this idea of not saying no to God, a phrase that we sometimes hear is, "I'm taking a break." Where in the Bible is it OK to take a break from God, from Jesus, from the church, from Christianity? When Demas took his "break," Paul said he loved the world. As far as we know, he never came back from this break. Yes, we understand there are times in everyone's lives when an adjustment of what they are doing and how they are doing it and when they are doing it is necessary. Yes, we must be wise in determining what kind of emotional and physical load we can and should carry. But in the end, it's never OK to say NO to God.

Concept 3: If It's Not Daily, It's Not Christianity

Jesus said if anyone would come after him, he must deny himself and take up his cross daily and follow him (Luke 9:23). Christianity is not a Sunday kind of thing or a some-of-my-days kind of thing. Every day is to be the adventure of striving to think, act, react, live and love like Jesus. So if it's not daily, it's not Christianity.

Concept 4: Understand the Seasons of Life

As there are different seasons in a year in which there are different focuses of our time and energy, there are also different seasons in life as we age. And during these times, we use our time and energy in different ways. There is the growing-up season of life when most of us live with our parents. There is the college season of life when many move out of the family home for the first time. There is the single season of life. That may be short or long depending on our desire and life situation. There is the young married season. There is the parents-of-young-children season. There are the stressful and demanding seasons of work. There are seasons of health issues. There is the teen season with your kids. There is the empty-nest season. There can be seasons of money issues. There can be seasons of marriage issues. There can be a season of grief and loss or a season of financial blessings. The point is, as we move through different seasons of life, there are different amounts of time needed for the responsibilities of that season.

For example, when we (Randy and Kay) were students at the University of Florida, we were both single, without children and without needing to work to pay our bills because we had parents who were willing to pay for our education. This left us with much free and discretionary time since we did not have to take time for the responsibilities of a spouse, children or making money to pay bills. This allowed us to spend a lot of time in fellowship and in building many Christian friendships. It allowed us much time for discipling relationships and much time in evangelism. As we have moved through different seasons that had different demands and responsibilities attached to them, we have had to make adjustments. The key thing to understand is that there can never be a season to not embrace in our lives the eight Specifics of Life. We can't balance our lives by throwing out something that God expects and commands. We balance our lives by figuring out how to use our time to fulfil all of our responsibilities effectively in any new season of life. At times, this will mean purging our lives of some nonessential commitments and activities to make room for the essential ones—the Specifics of Life.

RANDY: Several years ago I went through a season lasting three and a half years when I was not in the full-time ministry. During most of that time, I had a full-time job working with a structural-engineering firm. No, I am not a structural engineer; I was just a guy on the sales team selling to architects. So I was out of the full-time ministry and, of course, my schedule became very different. Although I couldn't study with as many people, I still shared my faith and taught people about Jesus. Although I could no longer have the flexibility to meet with brothers throughout the day, I met with a group of great brothers for study, prayer and fellowship one time a week very early in the morning before we all went to work. On the nights of our midweek church service, it was sometimes a rush to leave my work, pick up Kay from her job, get through the traffic, have a little something for dinner and then get to church on time. We were tired and didn't always stay after church for fellowship as long as we had in the past. But we found a way to embrace a very different season of life holding on to Jesus being our Lord.

Concept 5: Your Christianity Is Your Own Responsibility!

Each individual is to work out their own salvation. It's not the job of the leaders to get you to heaven! Now, they'll do everything they can, but it's primarily each disciple's responsibility. Certainly, leaders will give you the opportunities needed for you to grow and mature in your faith. They are to equip, protect and lead the flock. But in the end, you are to take the given opportunities and train yourself to be godly. You are to work out your salvation, which means you work out your schedule, your marriage, your family, your seasons of life! It's your job to figure out your life and to keep Jesus being the Lord of it.

Keep yourselves in God's love as you wait for the mercy of our Lord Jesus Christ to bring you to eternal life. (Jude 21)

Therefore, my dear friends, as you have always obeyed—not only in my presence, but now much more in my absence—continue to work out your salvation with fear and trembling. (Philippians 2:12)

But solid food is for the mature, who by constant use have trained themselves to distinguish good from evil. (Hebrews 5:14)

Have nothing to do with godless myths and old wives' tales; rather, train yourself to be godly. (1 Timothy 4:7)

Concept 6: Be Responsible but Not Over-Responsible

There are people who tend to try to carry too much of a load and there are those who don't try to carry enough of a load. According to the Scriptures, we need to learn to be the people who are willing to help others carry their load of life when it becomes so heavy that they are falling beneath it. And, at the same time, we need to carry our own load. No one should expect others on an ongoing basis to carry them through life. To overdo trying to help others is not love, but enabling.

Certainly some people have challenges and difficulties and pains that seem heavier than others, yet God expects everyone to ultimately figure out how to live their lives in such a way that they carry their own load of life and are even in the position to help others who are genuinely in need. This is made clear with the following scriptures:

> *Carry each other's burdens, and in this way you will fulfill the law of Christ....Each one should test their own actions. Then they can take pride in themselves alone, without comparing themselves to someone else, for each one should carry their own load.* (Galatians 6:2, 4–5)

In this passage, we are told to carry each other's burdens, then we are told that everyone should carry their own load. So again, both are true. There is a tension between the two commandments. A good illustration of this is when Paul teaches in 2 Thessalonians 3:10, *"The one who is unwilling to work shall not eat."* It is not unloving to refuse to help a brother who is in need of food if he is able but is unwilling to work. To give help (to carry another person's burden) in this case actually hurts them more than helps them. To help in this case would be to enable the laziness and irresponsibility to continue. So the loving thing to do would be to expect them to learn to carry their own load of life by not helping them with free food. As a disciple of Christ, don't be over-responsible for others. This would only wear you out and eventually emotionally bankrupt you. And don't be under-responsible. We are to help those who are in need—emotional needs, spiritual needs or physical needs—but we are not to carry people through life. We are to help them get to the point where they can deal with their own lives successfully. Therefore, we are to be responsible but not over-responsible.

Concept 7: Understand You Obey Your Highest Authority—God

The highest authority in our lives is God and his word. He has instituted other authorities we are to obey, but if they are in conflict, we are to obey God, who is our highest authority. There is parental authority with children: *"Obey your parents"* (Ephesians 6:1). There is husband authority with a wife: *"Wives should submit to their husbands in everything"* (Ephesians 5:22–24). There is civil authority over citizens: *"Be subject to the governing authorities"* (Romans 13:1). There is employer authority over employees: *"Obey your earthly masters"* (Ephesians 6:5–8). There is church leadership authority with the body of Christ: *"Obey your leaders"* (Hebrews 13:17).

When any authority asks us to do something, the question must be asked in our minds if God has said something different. If he has, we are to obey him, not our husband or parent or employer or church leader. For example, when Peter and John were told by the civil authorities to stop evangelizing, they said they must obey God rather than man:

> Then they called them in again and commanded them not to speak or teach at all in the name of Jesus. But Peter and John replied, "Which is right in God's eyes: to listen to you, or to him? You be the judges! As for us, we cannot help speaking about what we have seen and heard." (Acts 4:18–20)

In the same way, if an employer asks an employee to lie to a client, there must be a tactful refusal. If an unbelieving husband tells a believing wife not to go to church, she must respectfully say no. If someone in church leadership is expecting something unbiblical from a member, that member must appeal to the higher authority of God's word. Jesus made clear who the highest authority would be if a person became his disciple: *"If anyone comes to me and does not hate father and mother, wife and children, brothers and sisters—yes, even their own life—such a person cannot be my disciple"* (Luke 14:26).

The Greek word for "hate" is *miseó*. It is used on a comparative basis. It means to love less but in very strong terms. It means to denounce one choice in favor of another. But it does not mean that we love or denounce just a little less. The use of this word paints the picture that we are to love Jesus much, much more in comparison to even those we love the most in this life. The practical truth of this is that we will always please the one we love the most. As we live our lives to glorify God, to have Jesus as our Lord, to walk in love by embracing all the specifics or responsibilities of life, we must understand we are always to obey the highest authority in our lives—God.

Concept 8: Know, Welcome and Respect Boundaries

Boundaries are a good thing. Boundaries keep us safe. When we were told to not go out of the fenced-in yard as a young child, it was for our well-being, not to take away our freedom to roam the neighborhood. When a child is told not to use the foot-long butcher knife as a lightsaber to play *Star Wars* with other kids, the parent is not trying to take away his fun. The parent is only trying to keep both their child and their child's friends out of harm's way.

The boundary lines have fallen for me in pleasant places; surely I have a delightful inheritance. (Psalm 16:6)

God has given us boundary lines for our lives. There are so many places to go where we are free to roam and so many things to do in life that we are free to experience. But there are places we are not to go and things we are not to do in our lives. They are out of bounds! The key word about boundaries in this passage is *"pleasant."* We must feel and believe God's boundaries are pleasant and best and wonderful and wise. If we don't, we will desire to break out of God's boundaries because we will be thinking there is something better. For instance, there are boundaries on our sexual desires. This was discussed in Love Secret 9 to a great extent. The main issue here is in delighting, treasuring and holding dear God's boundaries believing he knows and desires what is best for us. When God takes something from your grasp, he's not punishing you, but merely opening your hands to receive something better. We are to know and welcome and respect boundaries.

Concept 9: Use Who You Are to Serve and Build Up the Church

All our talents belong to God. Whatever we are capable of intellectually or physically, God is the one who has given us that ability. A good rule of thumb is to take what your responsibility level is at your workplace and then ask yourself how you can serve in a similar responsibility level at church. If you can manage ten people at work, couldn't you lead a small group effectively for God? Can you use what you have been trained and educated in to serve the church? Are you a graphic artist? Are you an IT (Information Technology) person? Are you an architect? Are you a salesperson? How can your church benefit from the skills you have? We need to take who we are and what we love doing and figure out how to make the church better and more effective with our knowledge and talent. Our leaders are to equip us spiritually, but they are probably not best at what you do and have devoted your life to knowing. Everyone is needed and everyone is important to build up the body of Christ out of love.

> But remember the LORD your God, for it is he who gives you the ability to produce wealth. (Deuteronomy 8:18a)

> Each of you should use whatever gift you have received to serve others, as faithful stewards of God's grace in its various forms. (1 Peter 4:10)

> So Christ himself gave the apostles, the prophets, the evangelists, the pastors and teachers, to equip his people for works of service, so that the body of Christ may be built up....
> From him the whole body, joined and held together by every supporting ligament, grows and builds itself up in love, as each part does its work. (Ephesians 4:11–12, 16)

We are to use who we are to serve and to build up the church.

Concept 10: Don't Be Over-Wicked or Over-Righteous
There is a very interesting scripture found in Ecclesiastes.

> Do not be overrighteous,
>   neither be overwise—
>   why destroy yourself?
> Do not be overwicked,
>   and do not be a fool—
>   why die before your time?
> It is good to grasp the one
>   and not let go of the other.
> Whoever fears God will avoid all extremes. (Ecclesiastes 7:16–18)

Extremes are harmful to living an optimal life. Certainly this passage is not telling us that having some wickedness is good for us and having too much righteousness is bad for us. But it is saying that a wrong view of righteousness and wisdom can be a destroying factor for people. It can destroy our joy of living. It can destroy our relationships because the way we relate to life puts people off. It can destroy us because it causes us to carry a load of guilt and shame. It can destroy us emotionally by making us feel like we never do enough. It causes a person to be like some well-known characters from *Saturday Night Live:* Debbie Downer or the Church Lady. Debbie Downer portrays someone who is always saying things and doing things that put a damper on whatever is happening around her. The Church Lady goes around saying and doing things that makes people around her feel guilty or judged. The characters tend to see the bad and evil in life and in people instead of the good and the positive. To some degree, thinking like this will eventually destroy a person from the inside out as it steals away the fulfilling life God intends for all to have.

Being overly wicked leads to an early grave. What a waste of life! God wants us to enjoy our lives. God wants us to live productive lives. God wants us to live with a positive view of ourselves, of others and of life in general. We are to enjoy life without needing to find joy in doing what is sinful. We are to know that God provides everything for our enjoyment. We are not to feel guilty or bad for what we have, but we learn to use it correctly to help others. We enjoy the gift of life and the gift of our possessions and all the good things there are on this planet.

> *This is what I have observed to be good: that it is appropriate for a person to eat, to drink and to find satisfaction in their toilsome labor under the sun during the few days of life God has given them—for this is their lot. Moreover, when God gives someone wealth and possessions, and the ability to enjoy them, to accept their lot and be happy in their toil—this is a gift of God. They seldom reflect on the days of their life, because God keeps them occupied with gladness of heart.* (Ecclesiastes 5:18–20)

> *Enjoy life with your wife, whom you love.* (Ecclesiastes 9:9a)

However many years a man may live
let him enjoy them all. (Ecclesiastes 11:8a)

Command those who are rich in this present world not to be arrogant nor to put their hope in wealth, which is so uncertain, but to put their hope in God, who richly provides us with everything for our enjoyment. Command them to do good, to be rich in good deeds, and to be generous and willing to share. In this way they will lay up treasure for themselves as a firm foundation for the coming age, so that they may take hold of the life that is truly life. (1 Timothy 6:17–19)

There is much to do in this life but there is much to enjoy as we do it. We are to have a joyful demeanor in life. We are to enjoy our spouse who should be our best friend on the face of this earth. We are to have great, fun and memorable times with our children. We are to enjoy the company of disciples who are friends in every possible way. We are to have refreshing times reaching out and befriending others as we share Christ with them.

Let's now come to the conclusion of this chapter asking the same question we started with: What is the picture of our response to God? What is our response to his love supposed to look like? Or what are our lives as disciples, as Christians, supposed to look like? We hope you now have a very clear and beautiful picture of this in your hearts and minds. We will close with a story about a little boy named Bradley. When it comes to our response to God, we think this says it well!

One morning when eight-year-old Bradley came down to breakfast, he put a little piece of paper, neatly folded, on his mother's plate. His mother opened it, and could hardly believe it. This is what her son had written:

Mother owes Bradley:

For running errands	$5.00
For taking out the trash	$3.00
For sweeping the floor	$1.00
Extras	$1.00
Total Mother owes Bradley...	$10.00

His mother smiled when she read that, but she did not say anything. When lunchtime came she put the bill on Bradley's plate along with ten dollars. Bradley's eyes lit up when he saw the money. He stuffed it into his pocket as fast as he could and started dreaming about what he would buy with his reward.

All at once he saw there was another piece of paper beside his plate, neatly folded, just like the first one. When he opened it up, he found it was a bill from his mother. It read:

Bradley owes Mother:

For being good to him	nothing
For nursing him though sicknesses	nothing
For shirts and shoes and toys	nothing
For his meals and beautiful room	nothing
Total Bradley owes Mother...	nothing

Bradley sat looking at this new bill speechless. After a few minutes he got up, pulled the ten dollars out of his pocket, and placed it in his mother's hand. After that he served his mother because of love.

Now here's your bill from Jesus.

What you owe Jesus:

For bleeding for you	nothing
For healing you	nothing
For praying for you	nothing
For dying for you	nothing
For changing your life	nothing
For giving you eternal life	nothing
Total you owe Jesus...	nothing

When you understand this, you'll serve God because of love.

PART FIVE

CONQUERING LOVE

We are living in a sophisticated world. This is an age of incredible advances in science, technology, medicine and education. The availability of information is at our fingertips. Experts in every field abound. Knowledge is accessible for all who seek it. This all sounds great, right? It describes a perfect society with all the answers. But as we look around our world, we don't see many people living triumphant lives. On the contrary, we see people defeated by life. We see people overcome with frustration, depression, insecurity, loneliness, prejudice, envy and fear.

In all of history, there is only one human being who can model for us a completely victorious life. Only one who was perfect, and who perfectly loved. And of course that one is Jesus Christ. Because of the love of Jesus, we can share in his victory! As we come to the final part of our book on radical love, we can know that we have the answers to life and to love through Jesus. Don't be fooled into thinking that the solutions are found anywhere else. Consider the old Arab proverb:

> A person who knows not and knows not that he knows not is a fool—shun him.
>
> A person who knows not and knows that he knows not is a student—teach him.
>
> A person who knows and knows not that he knows is asleep—awaken him.
>
> But a person who knows and knows that he knows is a wise man—follow him!

We can paraphrase that proverb and most assuredly say:

> This world in its instructions on love knows not and knows not that it knows not; it is foolish—shun it!

The loving Christ who knows and knows that he knows is wise—follow him!

Those who have chosen to follow the way of Christ are following the way of love. It is because of that love that life can be victorious. We can be more than conquerors!

> *No, in all these things we are **more than conquerors** through him who loved us. For I am convinced that neither death nor life, neither angels nor demons, neither the present nor the future, nor any powers, neither height nor depth, nor anything else in all creation, will be able to separate us from the love of God that is in Christ Jesus our Lord.* (Romans 8:37–39, emphasis added)

The love of God in Christ Jesus is unconquerable by the world's downward pull. But why are the words *"more than conquerors"* used? The word used for this in the Greek is *hupernikao*. It's only found here in the whole Bible. The word is a combination of two words: *nikao*, which means to subdue, to conquer or to give victory; and *huper*, meaning over and above, beyond or more than. This passage gives those who follow Christ a description that is so superlative it takes two words to define it! To be a conqueror would surely be enough for most of us, but God wants for us to experience even more.

In history classes you may have learned about Alexander the Great. The Greek hero conquered civilizations and overcame enemies. But he won his battles against armies that were less powerful than his. He was indeed a conqueror, but he was not *more* than a conqueror! Your favorite sports team might be winning against weaker teams. They conquer, but they are not *more* than conquerors. But when you beat something or someone who has beaten you, ravaged you and dominated you over and over again, then you are *more* than a conqueror! Are you ready to stop Satan's victories in your life with a life of love? Are you ready to be more than a conqueror?

Conquering Love Defined

Jesus gave the perfect example of conquering love when he told the parable of The Good Samaritan. Before we read this passage, it's important to understand the great animosity between the Samaritans and the Jews. Hundreds of years previous to the time of Christ, the Israelite nation was divided into two separate governments. The Northern Kingdom of Israel, with its capital in Samaria, was idolatrous and materialistic, worshipping golden calves and setting up places of sacrifice away from the temple in Jerusalem. When the Northern Kingdom was attacked and conquered by Assyria, its citizens were displaced and foreigners entered the land. Those who did remain became a mixed race of Israelites and non-Israelites. They also practiced a mixed religion (syncretism). The seventeenth chapter of 2 Kings explains their exile and behavior very clearly, pointing out that *"even while these people were worshipping the Lord, they were serving their idols"* (verse 41).

Later, the Southern Kingdom (Judah) was overthrown by the Kingdom of Babylon. The citizens of Judah were also exiled, but after a period of time many of the Jews were allowed to return and rebuild their temple and their cities. These citizens of Judah considered themselves the "true Jews," and they looked at the inhabitants of Samaria as "halfbreeds." There was incredible distrust and racial hatred between the Jews and the Samaritans.

This hostility makes the story of The Good Samaritan even more compelling. In the eyes of an expert in the Jewish law, the tale of the Samaritan as "the good guy" and the priest and Levite as "the bad guys" could be compared to the Nazis being the good guys and Captain America being the bad guy.

> On one occasion an expert in the law stood up to test Jesus. "Teacher," he asked, "what must I do to inherit eternal life?"
>
> "What is written in the Law?" he replied. "How do you read it?"
>
> He answered, "'Love the Lord your God with all your heart and with all your soul and with all your strength and with all your mind'; and, 'Love your neighbor as yourself.'"
>
> "You have answered correctly," Jesus replied. "Do this and you will live."
>
> But he wanted to justify himself, so he asked Jesus, "And who is my neighbor?"
>
> In reply Jesus said: "A man was going down from

Jerusalem to Jericho, when he was attacked by robbers. They stripped him of his clothes, beat him and went away, leaving him half dead. A priest happened to be going down the same road, and when he saw the man, he passed by on the other side. So too, a Levite, when he came to the place and saw him, passed by on the other side. But a Samaritan, as he traveled, came where the man was; and when he saw him, he took pity on him. He went to him and bandaged his wounds, pouring on oil and wine. Then he put the man on his own donkey, brought him to an inn and took care of him. The next day he took out two denarii and gave them to the innkeeper. 'Look after him,' he said, 'and when I return, I will reimburse you for any extra expense you may have.'

"Which of these three do you think was a neighbor to the man who fell into the hands of robbers?"

The expert in the law replied, "The one who had mercy on him."

Jesus told him, "Go and do likewise." (Luke 10:25–37)

When posed the eternal query, Jesus answered the question with a question: "How do you read the law?" The expert's answer was met with approval from Jesus; he was given an A+! But being the lawyer that he was, the expert had more questions to ask *"to justify himself."* He seemed to bristle at the concept of loving his neighbor, and he wanted to check out just whom he needed to show love toward. So Jesus described the hapless victim who was robbed as he went along the treacherous path from Jerusalem to Jericho. Although the priest and the Levite, held in high honor among the Jews, were unwilling to stop and help, the Samaritan, that prickly enemy of the Jews, came to his aid. He had pity for the suffering man and gave of his time, his supplies and his financial resources to make sure he was cared for. He stopped what he was doing, sacrificing his own personal agenda. He bandaged the man with his own clothing. He disinfected his wounds with his own wine, and soothed them with his own oil. He placed the man on his own donkey. He paid for his rehabilitation time at the inn with his own money.

When Jesus asked the expert in the law to identify the "neighbor" in this story, he was answered with a seemingly grudging response: *"The one who had mercy on him."* Is it possible that he answered in that way to avoid using the term "the Samaritan"? Perhaps he shuddered at having to admit that one of that race could be held up as a good example. Jesus, however, called the expert not only to have respect for the Samaritan in the story, but also to imitate him: *"Go and do likewise!"*

In many ways we are faced with the same question that the expert faced. We have learned that our job in life is to love God and to love others. But who are the others? How much love can we give? We can't meet the needs of every person that crosses our path! Moreover, in this era of information overload, we are burdened by the needs of people we will never meet. Images of people suffering around the globe leave us overwhelmed and saddened. Although we are obligated to contribute and offer assistance to faraway people, that is no excuse to neglect those who are nearby. Our neighbor is the person that is in our sphere of influence, and when we love our neighbor, it is the total fulfillment of the law. The 600-plus Jewish laws of what to do and what not to do get fulfilled when we love. And that makes God totally and fully happy.

> Let no debt remain outstanding, except the continuing debt to love one another, for whoever loves others has fulfilled the law. The commandments, "You shall not commit adultery," "You shall not murder," "You shall not steal," "You shall not covet," and whatever other command there may be, are summed up in this one command: "Love your neighbor as yourself." Love does no harm to a neighbor. Therefore love is the fulfillment of the law. (Romans 13:8–10)

And what is more, God has provided you with a way to love your neighbor. He has given you the way to practice this conquering love every single day! How? God places you in a "factory" that manufactures within each person this conquering love. The "factory" puts you in contact with people who will become your neighbors. As you learn to love these people, you will have conquering love. Some of these neighbors will be just like you. Others will be so different that you'll have to stretch yourself to get to know them. They will be people from various walks of life. Some will be needy; others will be affluent. Some will be highly educated; others will be barely literate. Some will be dark-skinned; others will be light-skinned. Some will be young, and some will be old. Some might not speak your language. Some will be nice to you. Some might neglect you. Some may even hurt you. But every one of these neighbors has something in common: Jesus is their Lord. These are your neighbors. They are the ones God will use to teach you to love, to forgive and to be forgiven. They will teach you conquering love! What is this "factory" that produces this kind of love? It's the church.

God created the institution of the church so that we can learn how to love our neighbors! It is through the church that we can learn how to be like the Samaritan. We can't learn to love and be like Jesus without other people who have the same goal in life. It's only within the community of believers that we can develop as human beings who are committed to the high call of following Christ. Within the close family of brothers and sisters, we learn to love, to forgive and be forgiven, and to show acceptance to those unlike ourselves. We can't learn those things in isolation. The church is the "factory" that develops human beings, all sinners with plenty of baggage, into people that resemble Jesus. Through our interaction and interdependence on one another, we become who God created us to be. We are also blessedly connected with others.

Jesus looked forward to the church he would build. He told the disciples that even *"the gates of Hades will not overcome it"* (Matthew 16:18). He wasn't speaking of a building or a social organization. He wasn't preparing them for a club that people could join. He didn't long to create a meeting for people to attend. No, Jesus anticipated a true church: a community of men and women committed to him as their Lord and committed to the cause of love, people who would love one another as they would seek and love the lost. Only then would the church be something that couldn't be overcome, even by the forces of hell. The church would be people who were more than conquerors!

A few years ago, a young man visited for the first time a *more than conquerors* gathering—that is, he came to a church service. He was inspired to write about his experience, and this is his message:

WAS THAT CHURCH?
Unknown author/Adapted

"There must be some mistake,"
I thought as I followed my friend into the auditorium,
Trying to get my bearings,
Maybe even comprehend what was going on.

"You said we were goin' to church,"
My mind shouted as I watched them all pour in—
Seemingly hundreds of happy people.
All smiles and "hellos."

This gathering was about as somber as Mardi Gras.
I didn't see any dour churchgoing faces.
Didn't see anyone comparing outfits.
What the heck was going on here?

These folks seemed almost related.
They sat down right next to each other.
Was this some kind of funky family reunion?
It definitely wasn't church!

Just as I was looking for Candid Camera
The music started kickin' in—
The singers flat-out rockin' their performance—
The one in the middle looked like he might explode.

The people in their chairs were just as excited.
I heard three or four impromptu harmonies—
Everyone holding on to each other.
I couldn't help it; I was feeling good.

Then came a group of tag-team preachers,
Each one as pumped up as his predecessor.
These men really believed what they were saying.
I can spot a phony at 50 yards.

I know I should have listened more closely
To the words of the tag-team preachers,
But the way the congregation seemed to be connected by
some invisible clothesline
Is what really kept me enthralled.

It seemed like it was over in about five minutes,
And I was thinking to myself as we were leaving,
"This will be the absolute first Sunday service
I have ever left feeling better than when I went in."

Someday I'm going to summon the courage
To ask my friend if that was really church that we attended,
Because I've lived all over the world
And I have never been to a church like that!

Conquering Love Is Powerful

When disciples of Jesus love one another, there is incredible power. To see people from all walks of life meeting one another's needs and getting along is a testimony. It certainly was like that with those who first followed Jesus. Let's imagine some of the things that they might have had to wrestle with:

John (the young one): "You want me to love James? He's so much older than me!"
Simon (the zealot): "Love Matthew, the tax collector? Our personalities are so different!"
Andrew: "Love Peter? He's always getting us in trouble with his big mouth!"
Peter: "Love John? He likes to get so close. Do I have to hug him?"

Jesus had his hands full as he trained these men in love. On many occasions he had to remind them and rebuke them, but he knew they would come around. He knew that love would break down all barriers. In the end, the disciples came together with the message that changed the world.

We too, as his followers, have the same kind of conquering love in us! God has given us the power to love others. All barriers are broken down when we express love in various ways, depending on the need:

Verbal expression of love—Sometimes we think that "it goes without saying" but it doesn't! It's never redundant to express words of love to those in your life. Not only "I love you," although that's so valuable, but also words that explain why you love are important too. It doesn't have to be flowery or poetic. You can write it down in a note if that helps. But learning to say the words to someone face to face is one way to have conquering love.

Emotional expression of love—It means so much when someone knows you are feeling with them in their joy or their sorrow. This allows you to identify with those you love and to sympathize with them. Shedding tears with those who are hurting is powerful. Enjoying what others enjoy is powerful too! Celebrating when another celebrates lifts a person up, leaving them encouraged and feeling cherished. To have another person sharing in laughter and tears is another way to have conquering love.

Physical expression of love—We're all so connected, right? We have all kinds of electronic connections that make us feel loved, right? All the beeps and buzzes keep us close, right? Well, maybe to some degree they do. It's wonderful that we can see the faces of loved ones far away by means of technology, but that can never take the place of physical touch. Holding someone's hand or giving a hug creates a connection that the camera on your phone never can. In fact, it's even been shown scientifically that physical touch is good for our health. When we touch someone the nerve endings under the skin send messages to the brain. So a gentle hug tells the brain to slow down the release of the hormone cortisol. This process helps reduce stress in the body! Physical touching also allows your body to produce and release oxytocin, which is known as the "love hormone." This is reported to lower the risk of heart attack, fight fatigue, boost the immune system, help fight infections and ease depression. There is a saying by Virginia Satir, a respected family therapist, "We need four hugs a day for survival. We need eight hugs a day for maintenance. We need twelve hugs a day for growth."

These expressions of love don't solve all the problems of the world, but they make the problems a bit more bearable. Love is what helps people get through difficult and challenging times. Love is what makes the fun times even more enjoyable. When we love, we are tapping into the greatest power there is. We become more than conquerors!

Conquering Love Proclaimed

Love is what changes people's lives. This world is filled with almost 7.5 billion people. Just in one typical day like today, approximately 350,000 new souls come into our world. They all need love. They all need conquering love! As you have learned about the love of God, about the revelation of love in Jesus, and about God's love "secrets," it's now up to you to live in love and to share that love with others.

The very first followers of Jesus met incredible resistance in their message of love. In fact, many Christians were persecuted because of their faith. Some were tortured and killed, but they didn't let go of their love and devotion to Jesus. An old story is told about some of these Christians of the first century:

One group of disciples, when commanded by the Roman authorities to deny Jesus as Lord, refused to give in. The Roman soldiers led a group of forty out on a cold and icy night. They were ordered to remove their outer clothing and stand in the middle of a frozen lake. If they would agree to proclaim "Caesar is Lord," then they could come off the ice, their clothes would be returned to them and they could go home.

The forty huddled together while the soldiers waited by the side of the lake, warmed by a fire. After a short while, they heard the sound of joyful singing. In voices that carried across the ice, the words struck the soldiers with wonder:

Forty wrestlers wrestling for thee, O God,
Crying to thee, O God
To give us the victory!

One of the soldiers listened intently to the song, which they repeated over and over at different intervals through the night. He considered the devotion that these Christians shared. He thought of their love for Jesus and remembered the story of Jesus being whipped, cursed, spit upon, mocked, beaten and crucified because of sin—including his sin. He thought about the claim of being raised from the dead. He considered this God of love who sent his Son to save the world. He reflected on the love that he had seen in them for each other. His heart was moved, and he was transformed by the singing and the message it brought to his soul. As he pondered all these things, the song changed:

Thirty-nine wrestlers wrestling for thee, O God,
Crying to thee, O God
To give us the victory!

Hearing these words, the soldier assumed one of their number, probably one of the older, frail ones, had died. But soon he heard footsteps and the weakened voice of one of their number as he approached the fire. "Give me my clothes," he cried. "Caesar is Lord...just let me go home!"

The soldier faced the one man who had deserted his cause and his Lord. And then something astonishing happened. The soldier began to remove his own outer garments. "Here," he said. "You can have mine and I'll take your place." The other soldiers looked on in amazement as he stepped out onto the ice. When he looked back at the man who was deserting Jesus he said, "You see, I'd rather die for your Jesus than live for my Caesar!" He joined the others in the middle of the lake, and soon the song changed once again:

Forty wrestlers wrestling for thee, O God
Crying to thee, O God
To give us the victory!

We love that story. It illustrates so much. And now, the only scripture that we could possibly close this chapter and this book with is found in Romans 8. We have already quoted a portion of it. Let's read the whole thought. You may want to read it out loud!

> *What, then, shall we say in response to these things? If God is for us, who can be against us? He who did not spare his own Son, but gave him up for us all—how will he not also, along with him, graciously give us all things? Who will bring any charge against those whom God has chosen? It is God who justifies. Who then is the one who condemns? No one. Christ Jesus who died—more than that, who was raised to life—is at the right hand of God and is also interceding for us. Who shall separate us from the love of Christ? Shall trouble or hardship or persecution or famine or nakedness or danger or sword? As it is written:*
>
> > *"For your sake we face death all day long;*
> > *we are considered as sheep to be slaughtered."*
>
> *No, in all these things we are more than conquerors through him who loved us. For I am convinced that neither death nor life, neither angels nor demons, neither the present nor the future, nor any powers, neither height nor depth, nor anything else in all creation, will be able to separate us from the love of God that is in Christ Jesus our Lord.* (Romans 8:31–39)

Where Are They?

For centuries, the love of God has been proclaimed. It's now our turn to carry the torch.

So, where are the men and women of this generation who will stand amazed at the love of God? Where are those who will be desperate for Jesus? Where are the slaves of Christ? Where are those who will deny themselves daily and freely give their time, their talents and their money to the cause of Christ? Where are those who will be obedient even unto death? Where are his lovers—those who will go to school, go to work and go to the mission field to win souls for Jesus?

Where are the adventurers, the explorers, the pioneers who will go anywhere, do anything and give up everything? Where are those who will love their neighbors across the street and across the globe? Where are those who will be more than conquerors? Where are the men and women of this generation who will live the life of RADICAL LOVE?

We believe they are right here...we believe it's YOU!

Also available from www.ipibooks.com

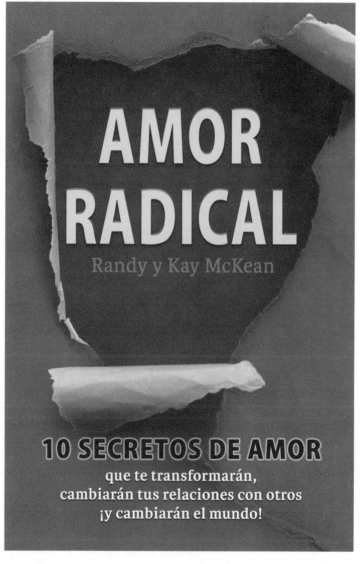

Amor Radical
10 Secretos de amor
Randy y Kay McKean
Price: $13.99

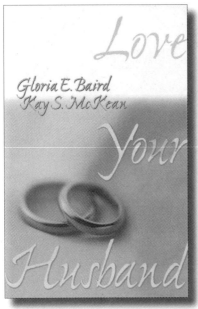
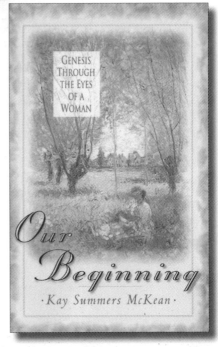

Also available from www.ipibooks.com

A Women's Ministry Handbook

by Jennifer Lambert and Kay Summers McKean

Price: $12.99

Also available from www.ipibooks.com

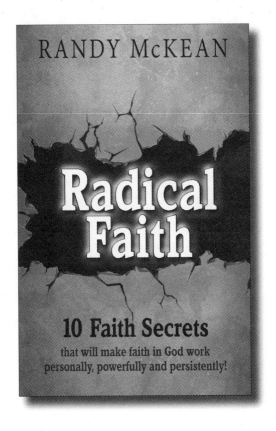

Radical Faith
10 Faith Secrets
by Randy McKean

Price: $13.99